R Quesnelt
P.7

876496

THE BUSINESS OF ENGLISH

THE BUSINESS OF ENGLISH

Judi Misener
Sandra Steele

TORONTO
OXFORD UNIVERSITY PRESS CANADA

Acknowledgements
We gratefully acknowledge the support of our families:
Bill and Tom, Erin, Meaghan, Andrew, and Matthew.

Canadian Cataloguing in Publication Data
Misener, Judi, date.
  The business of English

Includes index.
ISBN 0-19-540493-9

1. English language - Business English.
2. Communication. I. Steele, Sandra, date.
II. Title.

PE1115.M57 1986   808'.06651021   C86-094074-8

Project Editor: Muriel Fiona Napier
Editor: Sandra Richmond
Design: Joanna Gertler
Photo Research: Karen Clark
Illustration: Christine Alexiou
Compositor: Compeer Typographic Services Limited
Printed and bound in Canada by John Deyell Company

1 2 3 4 5 6 7 8 9 JDC 9 8 7 6

CONTENTS

9. THE BUSINESS OF REPORT WRITING / 213

JOB SEARCH IV — Getting Hired / 233

INTRODUCTION

Communication is an important part of everyone's life. But effective communication skills are even more important when you are working. In business and industry you will be dealing with many different types of communication. *The Business of English* will teach you the skills you need to communicate effectively in almost any work-related situation.

Most of the TAKE ACTION activities are based on circumstances you may encounter at work. If you are working part-time, or in a co-operative education program, TAKE ACTION ON THE JOB will enable you to use the business experience you are gaining now. As you work through all the activities, keep your "works in progress" and your completed assignments in a Business English Writing Folder your teacher will help you to start.

There are four special Job Search sections to help you apply the communication skills you learn to the very important business of finding a job. For example, you will use skills you learn in "The Business of Writing" when you compose a job application letter; you will use skills you learn in "The Business of Speaking" when you phone for a job interview.

The GETTING DOWN TO BUSINESS activities will form the basis of your personal Job Search Kit. Your Job Search Kit will reflect your interests and abilities, and will include such things as your résumé, a chart which lists possible job leads, sample letters of application, research on companies in which you're interested, and suggestions to help you communicate effectively in job interviews. When completed, your kit will cover all aspects of looking for a job—from helping you determine your career choices to exploring job leads, applying for jobs, being inter-viewed, and deciding whether a particular job is right for you.

NOTE
Some activities in this book require the use of material from other sources, such as television and radio programs, videotapes, films, and magazines. Whenever you wish to use such material, you must first obtain permission from the copyright holder.

The reproducible masters for the checklists and forms in this book are available in the Teacher Guide. It is your responsibility to obtain permission to reproduce and use forms provided by anyone else, such as a business or government agency.

THE
BUSINESS
OF
COMMUNICATION

1

Communication is a process
of sharing experience till
it becomes a common
possession.
JOHN DEWEY

TAKE NOTE
Communication occurs whenever you pass on a message to another person or other people. Your message could be verbal (spoken or written) or it could be non-verbal (e.g., a photograph, a drawing, an angry look, a nod of your head). Successful communication occurs whenever you send or receive a message that is clearly understood.

The ability to communicate well is one of the most important ingredients of business success and personal happiness. Very early in your life you made attempts to communicate effectively, to make others understand your messages. Your communication skills continue to improve as you learn from every new situation you encounter.

No matter what career you choose, you will have a "product" to sell all your life: your own capabilities and strengths as a person in both your private life and your professional life. Whatever your job, it will involve getting messages across to other people, whether they are your subordinates, your peers, or your bosses.

Most people think of communication as the sending and receiving of messages using words, either by speaking and listening or by writing and reading. Using words makes your communication **verbal**. However, **non-verbal** communication is often as important as verbal messages. You communicate non-verbally whenever you send a message without using words. Your message then may be contained in the expression on your face or the way you hold your body. Other forms of non-verbal communication include drawings, photographs, and charts.

THE COMMUNICATION MODEL

Every act of communication involves five ingredients:

- the sender
- the message
- the medium
- the receiver
- feedback

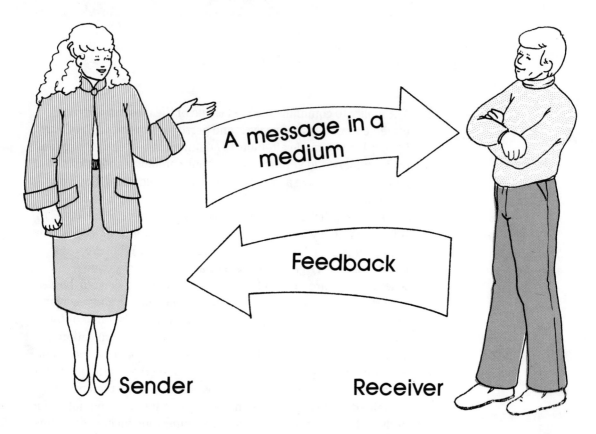

Sender

Receiver

Sender

The **sender** is the source of the communication process—the person with whom the message originates (e.g., the speaker, the writer, the painter).

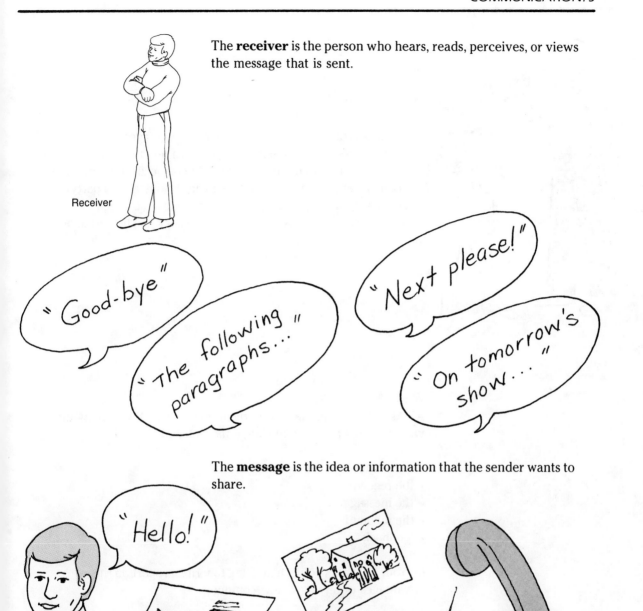

The **receiver** is the person who hears, reads, perceives, or views the message that is sent.

Receiver

"Good-bye"

"The following paragraphs..."

"Next please!"

"On tomorrow's show..."

The **message** is the idea or information that the sender wants to share.

"Hello!"

Dear Sir,

The **medium** is the means (form or format) chosen by the sender to transmit the message (e.g., speech, letter, picture).

Feedback is the receiver's response to the message. It can occur while the message is still being sent (a frown on the receiver's face that indicates lack of understanding) or it can occur soon after the message is sent (a thank-you note written the day after a party). Feedback is in itself a message but it is always a message in response to someone else's message. Feedback can be verbal or non-verbal; sometimes it can be both.

TAKE ACTION #1

A. As a class, examine each of the following situations involving various forms of communication and determine:

• the sender
• the receiver
• the message
• the medium
• feedback

(i) Your boss asks you in a meeting to write a report on the advantages of buying a new computer.

(ii) You receive an invitation in the mail to your cousin's wedding and you mail the reply card immediately.

(iii) The math teacher draws a diagram of an equilateral triangle on the blackboard to make a difficult problem clear to the class.

(iv) You smile brightly when you open your report card and discover to your surprise that you passed in your most difficult subject.

(v) Because you have the volume on your radio turned up, you can't hear your mother telling you that your best friend just telephoned.

B. Think of the various activities you were involved in yesterday at school, at home, or at work. Make a list of five attempts you made to communicate a message verbally to another person. Try to record the exact words of your messages, as well as any non-verbal messages that you sent while you were speaking.

GET THE MESSAGE?

In effective communication, the sender transmits a clear, concise, courteous, and complete message in an appropriate medium to a receiver who concentrates well enough to understand the message.

Sometimes, communication breaks down because one of the five ingredients—the sender, the message, the medium, the receiver, or the feedback—is defective in some crucial way. Whenever this happens there is a barrier to communication.

A barrier to communication occurs when an obstacle between the sender and the receiver blocks the message from being received and understood.

TAKE NOTE
Both the sender and the receiver contribute to the success or failure of almost all forms of communication.

BARRIERS TO COMMUNICATION CREATED BY THE SENDER
Sometimes the sender of the message unknowingly creates a barrier that blocks the message from being received and understood.

• **Using the wrong level of language** is one example of a barrier to communication. The language you use to speak or write to people in a position of authority is called formal language. You may also use formal language when speaking to a stranger or a group of people you do not know well. The language you use most of the time at school, on the job when speaking to your peers, or at home is informal language. The language you use when speaking to a friend who shares your knowledge of local, up-to-date slang is colloquial language.

Colloquial language is often direct and can be effective if the receiver understands the message. However, colloquial language is seldom appropriate in verbal business communications and is never appropriate in written business communications.

For example, there are different ways in which you might say goodbye or ask for a favour, depending on the situation.

Formal (to the woman you hope will hire you for a summer job):
"Good day, Ms. Hiring. I want to thank you for your time."
Informal (to your sister's new boyfriend):
"Goodnight, Gary. Hope to see you soon."
Colloquial (to your best friend):
"Gotta go. Catch ya later."
Formal (to your next door neighbour):
"Mrs. Jones, would you please ask your boarder to stop playing the radio so loudly? I have to study for a very important test."
Informal (to your mother, father, etc.):
"Mom, tell John to turn off that radio, I'm studying."
Colloquial (to your brother, sister, best friend, etc.):
"Hey, kill the noise! I'm hitting the books."

One of the secrets of effective communication is learning and using the correct language level in various communication situations. You would not, for example, ask your boss for a raise in the same way you would try to borrow money from a parent ("Gee Mom, couldn't you just give me ten dollars until payday?") or a friend ("I'm broke — can you lend me a couple of bucks?")

As a sender you should learn as much as you can about the receiver's personality, age, position in the community, and familiarity with local language customs, to suggest the level of language the receiver normally uses. Knowledge like this will help you choose the most appropriate language level for each situation and for each receiver of your messages.

TAKE ACTION #2

A. You have just witnessed an accident in the school parking lot. Now you have been called to the office to tell the principal what you saw. You will also be telling your favourite teacher and later still your best friend about the accident. Write three different versions of your story, choosing the appropriate level of language for each receiver or listener.

• **The disorganized thoughts of the sender** will also create a barrier to effective communication. Always take time to think of your purpose before you speak or write. Ask yourself, "What do I really want this person to do or understand?" Just speaking to keep the receiver's attention is a poor policy. Most people are very busy and appreciate a straightforward, well-organized message.

TAKE ACTION #3

A. Choose one of the five situations that you listed in TAKE ACTION #1 (B) (p. 7). Take time now to organize what you wanted to say and think about your purpose in communicating. Write down your message, changing the order of your words and ideas until you have achieved your purpose.

Would your new message be more effective?

• **Making your message too long or too short** is also a barrier to communication created by the sender. Too little detail can frustrate the receiver especially if, for example, the message is written and the sender cannot be questioned immediately.

Too much detail is often boring or insulting, and can waste a busy person's time. Again, knowledge of your receiver's age, education level, and awareness of, or familiarity with, the subject is crucial.

An example of too little detail might be a note from one of your parents simply saying, "Get supper". An example of too much detail might be a note on the same subject which includes the most minute details of instruction, such as "Take the hamburger out of the fridge and form it into patties. Butter the rolls found in the bread box and wrap them in tin foil . . ." This level of detail would be appropriate only if you had never made hamburgers for supper before.

TAKE ACTION #4

A. From the list you made in TAKE ACTION #1 (B) (p. 7), choose a situation in which you feel that you communicated successfully. Explain why the degree of detail that you gave the receiver was appropriate based on your knowledge of her or him. Now imagine that you are giving the same message to someone else, someone who knows considerably less about the subject involved. How would you have to change the message so that this receiver could understand? (For example, suppose your original message involved telling your best friend where to meet you in the mall where you both work. Your second message might be to give a friend who has never visited the mall instructions on how to meet you.)

• **Problems with the medium** used to transmit the message can create communication barriers. These problems can be caused by technology (e.g., a bad connection on a telephone line) or by using a medium that is not best suited for the message (e.g., reciting a long list of figures to someone rather than writing them down). Being aware of possible problems with the medium and understanding the purpose of your message can help you avoid these problems.

• **Sending information that is incorrect** creates a communication barrier. This problem is caused by insufficient research or dishonesty. The first problem sometimes leads to the second. Honestly admit if your information is incomplete; never make up an answer and pass it off as factual. Your personal credibility is at stake.

BARRIERS TO COMMUNICATION CREATED BY THE RECEIVER
When you are the receiver of a message, you may unknowingly create barriers that will prevent the message from being received and understood.

• **Lack of concentration** causes many receivers to miss the message. As a listener, reader, or viewer you must make an effort to concentrate. Self-discipline is required to eliminate outside distractions.

TAKE ACTION #5

A. In the situations described below some distraction hinders your ability to concentrate. Explain what you would do to improve your chances of receiving the message.

(i) You answer the telephone and quickly realize that the connection is so bad that you can hardly hear the person who has called.

(ii) Your boss is giving you instructions for the next day when she will be away but you can hardly hear her because noisy repairs are being done in the hall next to your office.

(iii) You are reading a very important section of your history textbook when you realize your eyes are extremely tired and strained. It is 11:30 p.m. The passages must be read for a 9:00 a.m. class.

• **A poor attitude** towards the situation or the sender often causes the receiver to miss the message. If the message is important to you, you will have to concentrate on it and not on how you feel about its content or the sender.

TAKE ACTION #6

A. Everyone hates to admit to suffering from a poor attitude but in certain situations we all do. For example, although you may not want to listen to your dentist as he tells you that your tooth must be pulled, it is important to your good health that you listen carefully. Working in groups, describe one situation or person in your life that causes you to have a negative attitude. Discuss how you can overcome your negative attitude in order to become a more efficient and effective receiver.

• **Lack of understanding** can create a barrier to communication. If a clear, well-organized message has been sent, why wouldn't you get the message? These are the most common reasons:

— You are not familiar with the language that was used. (e.g., it was too technical, contained jargon you don't use or words you haven't heard before).

— You are not familiar with the subject (e.g., the sender assumes you know all about computers and launches into a discussion that leaves you shaking your head in confusion).

THE ROLE OF FEEDBACK

Your sensitivity to the importance of feedback, both verbal and non-verbal, will improve your skills as both a sender and receiver of messages. When you send messages, you should look for feedback from the receiver to assure you that your message has been understood or to alert you to the need for clarification. If there is no feedback, you cannot assume the message has been received and understood. You should always confirm that in fact the receiver has "got the message." When you receive messages you should use feedback to tell the sender whether you understand.

This particular communication barrier is most likely to arise in an oral communication situation. Becoming more aware of the power of feedback will make you a better communicator.

TAKE ACTION #7

A. As a class, read the following and identify any barriers to communication you think are present. Explain how the barriers could be overcome.

(i) You find the following note on your desk: "Your boss called to say meet the plane at 10 o'clock."

(ii) You receive a letter from a customer requesting the specifications for a new computer system. Your supervisor decides you don't have time to type a letter and asks you to phone the information to the customer. Two weeks later your manager receives a letter from the customer complaining that he was given the wrong figures.

(iii)

okay

Dear Ms. Goldman:

I was delighted to hear the news yesterday. It's so gratifying when companies such as yours realize the worth of dedicated and resourceful personnel.

I look forward to working with you over the coming months. Congratulations on your promotion.

Yours sincerely,

C. Hatanaka

C. Hatanaka

(iv)

– level of language
  too long
S.– conwdent
   appropriate
   eliminate
   unimportant
R – can't do
   anything

Dear Customer:

I am sorry to report that the part you ordered from us on the 25th of March is not in stock. I have personally checked the store room and queried the managing director who informs me that he hasn't the foggiest notion of when we may expect delivery from our supplier.

Thus I must regretfully inform you that your order cannot be filled at this time. However, I will drop you a line as soon as I have more information about the availability of this item.

Yours truly,

Rick Richardson

Rick Richardson
Sales Manager

concentration (v) You can't hear the speaker at a lecture because the audience is too noisy.

attitude (vi) Your supervisor asks you to do something you think will be extremely boring. Your answer to your supervisor is "Oh, come off it." Two days later you receive a termination notice.

okay (vii) *Switchboard*: J&S Manufacturing. Good morning.
Caller: Hello. May I speak to the manager please?
Switchboard: I'm sorry—she's away at a meeting all day. Could someone else help you?
Caller: No, thank you. Could you have her call me tomorrow? It's Jean Ladouceur at 555-9872.
Switchboard: Certainly, Mr. Ladouceur. I'll have her call you at 555-9872.
Caller: Thank you. Goodbye.

(viii)

— too short
— no detail

> Dear Customer:
> The item you ordered is not in stock.
>
> *F. Rutherford*
>
> F. Rutherford
> Manager

(ix)

disorganized

> Dear Sir or Madam:
> This is to inform you my family allowance cheque should be increased, as I have just given birth to twins in the enclosed envelope.

RULES FOR SENDERS

As a sender, you should:

- try to find out as much as possible about the receiver. This helps you decide the appropriate level of language to use and the necessary amount of information for your message.

- plan your message. To do this you must be aware of the purpose of the message. Planning ahead of time can help you send an organized, clear, concise, and accurate message.

- be aware of the importance of the medium. Using the most appropriate medium and being aware of potential problems can help make your communication more effective.

- look for and expect feedback from the receiver. This ensures that your message has been received and understood or lets you know that it needs to be clarified.

RULES FOR RECEIVERS

As a receiver, you should:

- try to find out as much as possible about the sender. Being aware of the sender's background and the purpose of the message leads to more effective communication.

- remove any distractions which might hinder your ability to concentrate on the message.

- try to overcome negative feelings towards a situation or sender so that you can understand the message.

- give feedback to the sender. Letting the sender know that you need more information or acknowledging that the message has been received and understood is essential to effective communication.

NON-VERBAL COMMUNICATION

> TAKE NOTE
> Non-verbal communication is as important as verbal communication. It can clarify, reinforce, or even contradict what is being said, or it can communicate a complete message by itself.

Non-verbal communication, or sending a message without using words, is one of the most fascinating forms of communication. We communicate non-verbally through such things as body language, appearance, voice control, and graphics.

What other ways can you think of in which we communicate non-verbally?

BODY LANGUAGE
Body language is the manner in which we communicate using:

- facial expressions
- eye contact
- body posture
- gestures of the hands, arms, feet
- distancing

TAKE ACTION #8

Facial Expressions

A. Examine the pictures on p. 18 and decide what type of message is being sent. Make a list of the facial features that helped you decide what the message was (e.g., raised eyebrows—look of surprise).

B. Some people have very expressive faces. Their faces easily show what they are thinking and the emotions they are feeling. When you are at home tonight, watch yourself in a mirror as you try out different facial expressions. Try expressions to demonstrate anger, fear, happiness, sadness, puzzlement, interest, and curiosity. (Lock your door or your family might think you've developed a strange habit!)

Eye Contact

C. Have you ever talked to someone who does not look at you? Do you look away when someone talks to you? Think about conversations you have had where you looked someone in the eye as you spoke. How did that person react?

D. With a partner, begin a conversation on a subject which interests you both. Look each other in the eye. How do you feel? Now talk to each other back-to-back, then side by side, then, once again, face to face. As a class discuss how you felt in each situation.

Body Posture

E. During your classes today, watch how your fellow students make use of posture and distance in communication situations. If a student is being reprimanded what happens? If a student is being praised or spoken to in a positive way what happens?

Gestures

F. Do you know people who talk with their hands or move their knees up and down when seated? As a class, make a list of gestures used in everyday conversations and discuss why people use them and how they might be interpreted.

G. Are you familiar with the interpretation of gestures and expressions used by people who are not originally from the North American culture? Different cultures interpret non-verbal communication differently. As a class, share your knowledge of other cultures.

Distance

H. There is also a definite pattern to how we distance ourselves when talking to others. Research has indicated that these are North Americans' usual distance zones:

intimate distance	15 to 45 cm
personal distance	46 to 120 cm
social distance	1 to 3.5 m
public distance	3.5 to 4.5 m

Where do you stand when talking to each of the following: your teachers, your family, your friends, and strangers? Draw a diagram similar to the one below and place the people you come into contact with today in the various distance zones. Analyse your diagram. Is there a pattern about the distance you prefer to place between yourself and others? Does the distance vary depending on whether you are the receiver or sender?

| intimate 15 to 45 cm | personal 46 to 120 cm | social 1 to 3.5 m | public 3.5 to 4.5 m |

I. It is important that you read the body language that tells you whether you are too close to the person with whom you are communicating. If you are too close, your receiver might start to fidget or move away from you — both signs of discomfort.

Spend a day changing your normal distance zones. For example, stand far away from someone you usually stand close to or ask one of your teachers if you can change your seat in class. Record how you changed distances and how you felt when you did. Also record how people reacted when you made the changes.

J. Ask your teacher to show the class an old silent film. Observe the exaggerated facial expressions and gestures. Discuss as a class how the actors were able to tell their stories. What effect does the music have on the message which is being sent?

APPEARANCE

While you were doing the previous activities you were most likely subconsciously affected by another form of non-verbal communication—appearance. You might have made some decisions about the people with whom you were communicating.
You might have decided:

- how much you liked them.
- how smart you thought they were.
- how comfortable you felt talking to them.
- whether you would like to talk to them again.

How you take care of your own appearance also tells people a great deal about how you regard yourself.

First impressions do make a difference, especially in business, but what is considered appropriate may vary from company to company. What does your appearance tell others about you?

TAKE ACTION #9

A. Advertisers carefully plan every detail of an advertisement to create a powerful effect on the viewer—nothing is left to chance. The use of non-verbal communication is highlighted every second. Your teacher will show you some television advertisements. Watch the advertisements without the sound. Describe the appearance of the people and the message that their appearance sends to you.

B. Bring in a variety of pictures from newspapers and magazines for your class to "read". Write down your interpretation of each, then discuss the interpretations as a class. Did everyone interpret the same pictures the same way? Which major components of each picture influenced your interpretation?

C. Do you dress differently at home and at school? As a class discuss why people dress the way they do and the meaning of the saying, "The clothes make the person."

D. List five occupations which require a uniform. Why do these occupations require uniforms? What message does the uniform convey to you? Discuss the advantages and disadvantages of wearing a uniform to school.

VOICE CONTROL

Voice control describes how you use your voice when you speak, regardless of the meaning of the words you are speaking. Voice control includes:

- pitch
- intonation
- voice quality
- pace
- clarity
- volume

Every musical instrument produces a particular sound. If you imagine your voice is the sound produced by a very complex instrument (your vocal cords) then you will find it easy to understand what voice control is all about.

Think about a guitar. When you tighten a string on a guitar, the sound produced by that string rises in **pitch**. In the same way, when you tighten your vocal cords, the sound produced is at a higher pitch. Your vocal cords are muscles and although you are not aware of doing so, every time you speak you are tensing and relaxing them many times.

You will be most effective when speaking if you use your natural voice—which means you must find your natural pitch. Here is a simple exercise to help you do that—yawn three times, sigh three times, then say your name and address. You will have found your natural pitch.

The tune produced when you play a guitar consists of a number of different sounds formed into a particular pattern. Similarly, every time you speak you are unconsciously creating your own tune with your voice by varying the notes which you use. This is known as **intonation**.

Some guitars, depending on their size and the materials from which the body and strings are made, have a warm, resonant quality. Others, for the same reason, can sound thin and hard. This variation is also true of voices. The length of the vocal cords and the degree of tension in the muscles of the neck have a very noticeable influence on the **quality of the voice**. While obviously you cannot change the length of your vocal cords, you can work to gain greater control of the neck muscles and thus enhance the quality of your voice.

The **pace** at which you speak has a direct effect on your listener. Think about your own reactions when you have been the receiver of a verbal message from somebody whose rate of speech was extremely fast. Think of the opposite situation. Is it easier to understand someone who speaks slowly or someone who speaks quickly? Is there an ideal pace for everyday verbal communication?

The more clearly you speak, the more likely it is that your verbal message will be received and understood. **Clarity** is one of the areas of voice control where you can fairly easily identify problem areas in your own speech and make a deliberate effort to improve. For example, if you are in the habit of speaking quickly, you may find that some of your words tend to run together. You can make your message clearer simply by speaking more slowly.

The **volume** at which you speak should be a conscious decision on your part based on the communication situation. Your decision as to volume is based on the simple fact that your purpose in communicating is to make sure your message is received and understood. If the volume of your speech is such that your voice cannot even be heard, then obviously you are not communicating successfully. While your choice of volume should be deliberate, it is not always so. Your emotions can affect the volume of your voice. It is a good idea to practise "volume control" so that you do not allow this to interfere with effective communication.

TAKE ACTION #10

A. There are many ways a simple phrase can be said. Varying your intonation can result in a very different message being sent although the words remain the same. Try saying "I did" first as a question then as a statement of fact. What happens to the intonation in your voice in each case? Try saying "Good morning," "Great," and "Thanks a lot" using various intonation patterns. How does the change in intonation change the message being sent?

B. Placing more emphasis on one particular word in a sentence can change the meaning of the message as well. For example, try saying "I never said he stole the money" placing the emphasis on different words each time. How does the difference in emphasis change the meaning of the sentence?

C. As a class, compile a list of the emotions and feelings which are portrayed by speaking softly and by speaking loudly. Discuss how changing the volume in any particular case might alter the impact of your message.

D. As you walk through the halls today, listen to the volume of speech of your fellow students and your teachers. Make a note of examples where the use of change in volume was effective in getting a message across.

E. How do you interpret the message of someone who speaks rapidly compared with that of someone who speaks very slowly? List different situations that can affect the rate at which you speak.

GRAPHICS

Non-verbal communication also takes place through the use of graphics and symbols. The old saying that a picture is worth a thousand words has perhaps begun to suffer from over-use. But it is still true that a photograph, for example, can often communicate as well as or better than a written message.

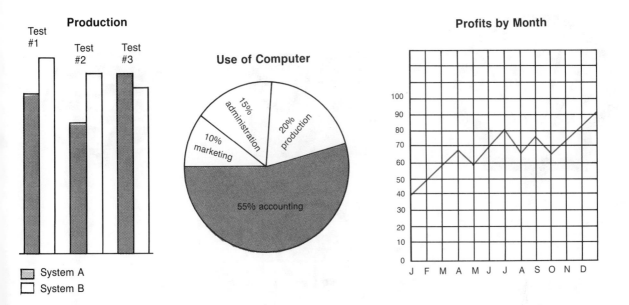

Written reports very often include charts and graphs without which they would not be as easy to understand. Indeed the information might not be complete without them.

It's becoming easier every day to travel quickly between places which are thousands of miles apart and often in different countries. Because of this we now have various international symbols which are recognized worldwide no matter what the viewer's country of origin.

AIR CANADA

Most companies nowadays, regardless of their size, have a special corporate logo. Many of these too are recognized internationally.

TAKE ACTION #11

A. Look back over the photographs, graphs, charts, symbols, and logos on the preceding pages and decide exactly what message is being sent by each of them.

B. Make a class list of graphics that you all see on a daily basis and decide what message is being sent by each of them.

C. Working in small groups, decide on a particular type of product your group is going to research (e.g., cars or soft drinks). Search through various magazines and papers to gather advertising material for your product. Work together to make a list of all the non-verbal communication techniques that are used. If your particular product also has television commercials, make a list of the additional non-verbal techniques in them. Decide why the advertisers used these particular techniques. How effective were they?

TAKE ACTION ON THE JOB #1
A. Does your place of business have a dress code? What is it and why is it in place?

B. Do people in your place of business dress differently depending on what type of job they do? What are the differences and why do they exist?

Communicating effectively is the most important aspect of your job search. Even if you have the exact skills an employer requires, you won't get hired unless you are able to get that message across.

In the Job Search sections you will use all the techniques you study in the various chapters of the book. By the time you have finished these sections you will have a complete Job Search Kit which is tailored to your abilities and interests. Your completed kit will contain information and strategies which you will be able to use to find whatever type of job you're seeking—part-time, summer, co-operative education, or permanent. Your Job Search Kit will be separate from the writing folder you are keeping throughout the course.

JOB SEARCH I
Getting Set

Read the following article from *The Edge*, then discuss it as a class.

FINDING A JOB

MAKING UP YOUR MIND

There are many reasons for wanting to work. To earn money, gain experience, and pursue lifelong ambitions are simply a few of the reasons why people seek jobs, hold them, and then change them.

No matter what your motives are for wanting to work, the first step towards finding a job is to take a long, hard look at yourself and the job market. Be as honest and objective as you can, and take the time to explore these questions:

- ☐ Why do I want to work?
- ☐ What are my immediate and long-range goals?
- ☐ What are my talents and skills?
- ☐ What are my shortcomings?
- ☐ What kinds of jobs and salaries can I reasonably expect to be offered in my local market?
- ☐ Should I move to another area to improve my prospects?
- ☐ How many different kinds of jobs could I possibly do that I would find rewarding?

Once you've asked yourself these questions, ask yourself again. Put your answers in writing — it may help you to articulate your feelings and give you a more objective view of yourself. Be absolutely sure about what you want and why.

If you have answered these questions in an honest and confident way, you will know what kind of job and salary to pursue. You will also have a head start on your personal interviews, because these questions will certainly be asked by people in a position to hire you.

After you've taken stock of both yourself and the job market, the next step is to prepare yourself for the demanding and time-consuming process of looking for a job. In many cases, it takes weeks, even months to get an offer. So while you are reading Want Ads, sending letters, and going to interviews, keep in mind that if someone cannot give you a job, it does not necessarily reflect a shortcoming of yours.

Don't take rejection to heart. Instead, believe in yourself. Keep your spirits high. Be persistent. Write letters and ask for interviews even when you suspect your chances are slim. Although there may be no opening at the time, people will remember your perseverance and positive attitude when a job does become available. Even if you are not ultimately successful, at least you will have the satisfaction of knowing you are doing everything possible for yourself.

If you continually project a positive and enthusiastic attitude, you will be improving your chances of getting a job by a hundredfold. Don't forget that when there are many applicants with essentially the same skills and qualifications, it could very well be your attitude that gives you the decisive edge over the others.

Now, what should you do if you are offered a job that is not related to your career goals? Consider it carefully! It could be the only offer you will get.

Remember that in an important sense every job is related, and any job can work for you if you want it to. A job of any sort will not only put money in your pocket, but will give you one of the most valuable commodities in the job market: experience.

When you look for a job again, it will be to your advantage to be able to show that you have held a responsible position at least once before. This could be the deciding factor that finally gets you the job that you think is ideal for you.

Before you embark on your job search, decide at the outset to be determined, optimistic, and flexible. Be firm in your commitment to do everything possible to get what you want, rather than sitting around hoping for some lucky accident to happen.

Getting the message across to an employer that you are the ideal candidate for a job depends on making your message the correct one. You must know your own abilities before you can convince an employer that you match what is needed on the job.

GETTING DOWN TO BUSINESS #1
A. (i) Using the following examples as a guide, make a list of your skills and abilities. Be resourceful—don't concentrate only on skills you may have gained in previous employment. Volunteer work, hobbies, and club memberships may have helped develop skills you may not be aware you possess.

Skill	Where learned	Performance Rating
photography	high-school club	beginner
typing	school course/summer office job	50wpm
small appliance repair	self-taught	help out neighbours and friends
dealing with public	part-time cashier grocery store	excellent
organizational/planning/ supervisory	volunteer work (day care centre); drew up work schedules and supervised implementation	fair

(ii) Discuss your list with a partner and try to suggest ways in which you each might add to the skills you've identified. For example, if your partner has listed typing as previous work experience, discuss what other skills and abilities this job may have required. Typing might also have meant proofreading and filing.

B. (i) Hold a class discussion and identify a number of careers in which various members of the class are interested. From the list you have created, or depending on your own interests, choose up to three jobs which particularly appeal to you. You are going to investigate these jobs and try to match them up with your own skills. Discuss with your teacher possible avenues you might explore and people you might talk to, to gather information.

(ii) Using a copy of the following chart, gather as much information as you can.

CAREER EVALUATION CHART

SKILLS

e.g., Does the career require that you be able to operate a microcomputer? Does the career require that you hold a licence to drive heavy machinery?

_____
_____

TRAINING

e.g., Does the job require special training that is not provided on the job?

_____
_____

OPPORTUNITY

e.g., Are there jobs in this field now? Will there be jobs when you are actively seeking employment?

_____
_____

ENVIRONMENT (WORKING CONDITIONS)

e.g., Does the job require you to work outdoors? Does the job require you to work in noisy conditions?

_____
_____

OPPORTUNITY FOR ADVANCEMENT

e.g., Does the job offer you chances for promotion?

_____
_____

SALARY/WAGES

e.g., What is the average salary in this field? Would it provide for your needs?

_____
_____

WORKING HOURS

e.g., Are they regular? Does the job involve shift work?

_____
_____

JOB SECURITY

e.g., Is there job security in this field?

_____

_____

WHAT THE JOB INVOLVES

e.g., What are the typical duties of this job?

_____

_____

TEMPERAMENT

e.g., Is this job best suited to a creative person or is it best suited to a person who prefers close supervision?

_____

_____

Once you have gathered sufficient information on the job(s) you have identified as being of interest to you, compare the material with what you identified in activity A as your skills, abilities, and interests. Consider the following questions:

- Are you still interested in the job(s) you identified?
- If so, how do your skills, interests, and abilities match?
- If they don't match, how could you develop the necessary skills?

Answer the questions either in point-form notes or in a brief paragraph. Discuss your answers with a partner and/or your teacher. Once you are satisfied that your answers are final, file them in your Job Search Kit.

C. Make a special folder into which you can put a collection of materials that you are reading to help you find a job. Include:

- articles about your chosen career field
- articles about job search tactics
- pamphlets you obtain from guidance counsellors, employment agencies, etc.

THE
BUSINESS
OF
ORGANIZERS

2

All things are beautiful as
long as you get them in the
proper order.
JOHN GRIERSON

TAKE ACTION #1

A. Make a list of how you organize various things in your life, such as your records, tapes, books, free time, and correspondence. As a class, discuss your choices and see if you can identify any patterns. Are they effective? Why are they necessary?

There are many ways of organizing what we communicate into a particular pattern which makes the message clearer and more easily understood. Whenever you listen and read, your role as a receiver is to look for the patterns used in the message that will help your understanding and recollection of the information. Whenever you speak or write, your role as a sender is to organize your messages effectively so that they can be understood and remembered easily.

The alphabetical filing system is one of the most common organizers used in business.

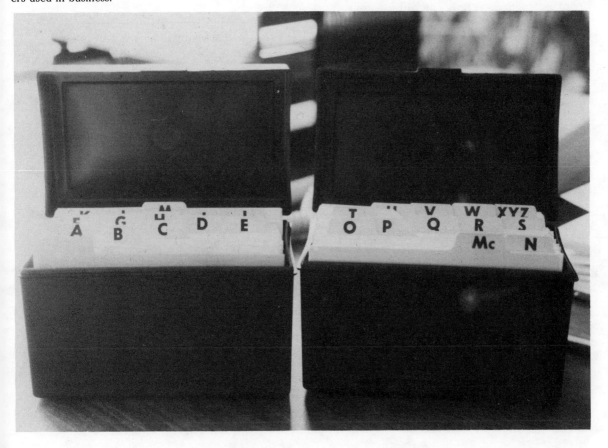

The following are some of the most common organizers used in sending messages:

ORGANIZER	EXAMPLE
Simple Listing –usually alphabetical or numerical	–alphabetical listing of a company's employees
Time Order –according to the order in which things happen	–instructions on how to load paper into a computer printer
Cause and Effect –giving reasons for and results of an action	–a report on the negative effects of second-hand smoke in the workplace
Comparison/Contrast –comparison points out both similarities and differences of two or more things; contrast points out only the differences	–a report on which of several word processors the company should buy
Spatial Order –how objects are arranged in a certain space	–the layout of shelving in a library in order by Dewey numbers
Order of Importance –from highest to lowest priority or vice versa	–a list of phone numbers with the most frequently called numbers at the top
General to Specific/ Specific to General –making a general statement and then giving specific examples or vice versa	–a credit card brochure stating that several payment plans are available and outlining each of them
Pros and Cons –presenting arguments in favour of (pro) and against (con) a certain action	–a report to a company's financial committee investigating the option of computerizing the payroll system

TAKE ACTION #2

A. Examine the following and identify the pattern used to organize the information. As a class, discuss whether the organizer used is effective and why. Could other organizers have been used?

(i)

The new Brand X personal computer is here. It's user friendly and it's compatible with most other systems. It has more than one hundred programs already written. And best of all, it costs less than any other personal computer on the market.

order of importance

(ii)

CALL TRANSFER
1. Depress hookswitch or Link button...hear
   3 beeps and dial tone, your party is on hold.
2. Dial desired party.
3. Announce call.
4. Replace handset.
NOTE: If the transfer is not accepted wait for the
second party to hang up, you are automatically
reconnected to the original party. If the extension
number you dialed is busy or there is no answer,
depress hookswitch or Link button to return to
original party.

fine

From *SL-1 Regular Telephone Manual*, Telecommunications Terminal Systems (TTS)

(iii)

We give you low prices, high quality,
and friendly service. We pride ourselves
on our commitment to our customers.

specific *general*

(iv)

MEMO

To: Employee   Date: Today
From: Boss
Re: Work to be done during my absence.

Make sure the final draft of the Atkins report
is done by Wednesday. Type up the agenda for
the next production meeting and start the word
processing project. If you have time at the end of
the week, check the inventory printout and catch
up on the filing.

important

less important

(v)

alpha

Stock	Sales	High	Low	Close	Net Ch'ge
ABS res i	4000	30	27	27	−3
AIS res i	2500	225	225	225	+5
Abaton j	8100	105	101	105	+4
Aby inv b j	32500	40	36	38	−1
Aber res i	25000	100	90	100	+10
Abo res	12000	48	48	48	+3
Acacia i	20000	25	25	25	+1
Acheron	20250	35	33	33	−1
Achilles i	1500	36	36	36	−1
Ad com i	3000	41	40	40	−4
Ad dome i	16000	35	35	35	−1
Adams ex i	2000	30	30	35	+1
Adola i	5000	22	20	21	−1
Agincourt i	500	70	70	70	−1
Airborne i	800	170	160	160	+2
Ajax res i	31000	360	345	345	−10
All star i	6000	48	48	48	−5
Allanco i	34550	56⅛	55⅞	6⅛	−2
Allure rs i	2000	60	60	60	+1¼
Altar gold i	5000	52	52	52	−5
Amark	117950	300	245	265	+1
Amble res i	20900	110	102	102	−25
Amca res	8800	145	138	145	−10
Amcan i	122833	215	185	145	+5
Amer bio i	2208	$7⅜	6¼	186	+6
Amer pltn i	6100	225	215	6½	−⅛
Amer tec i	500	63	63	223	+13
Am vol i	1000	16	16	63	+4
Ameroil i	16500	66	60	16	+4
Amir mine i	1500	98	98	65	−1
Anchor gld i	4500	70	63	98	+2
Anglo cdn	5000	69	69	70	+10
Anina res i	18500	96	92	69	+9
Ansco bc i	5000	33	33	96	+4
Arbor res	9158	320	300	33	+3
Archr mnr i	5000	90	86	320	+30
Argenta i	8400	225	200	90	−5
				200	−30

(vi) spatial

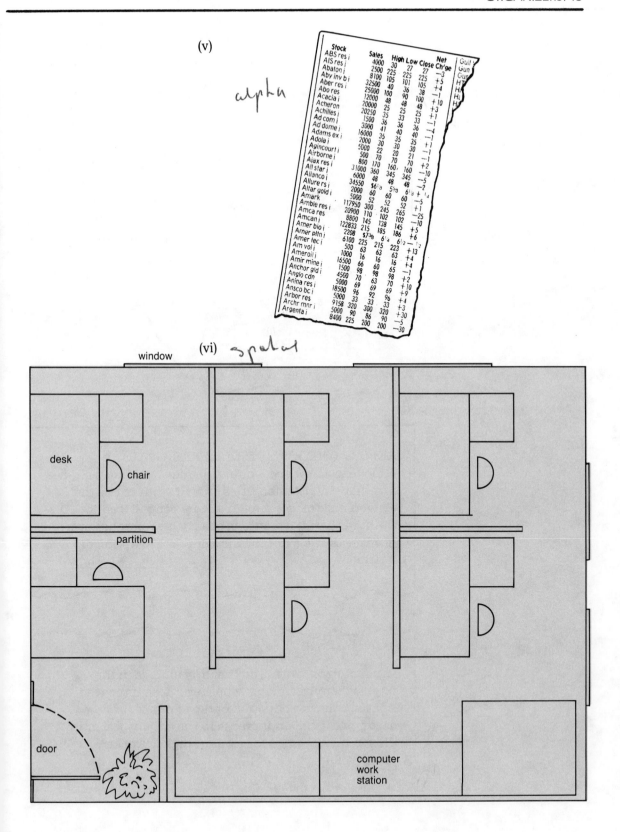

window

desk

chair

partition

door

computer
work
station

(vii)

compare/
contrast

ITEM	CAR A	CAR B	CAR C
power steering	X	X	X
power brakes	X	X	X
front wheel drive	X		X
automatic transmission	X	X	X
air conditioning		X	
sun roof	X		
X means item is available			

(viii)

general
~~specific~~

Clerical help required for small
office. Must have accurate typing,
good telephone manner, some
bookkeeping experience.
Call 555-6907. *specific.*

(ix)

pro

REPORT ON NEW BUILDING PROPOSAL
A move to a new site would provide us with more space
and more modern facilities as well as giving us the
convenience of working in a more central location. On
the other hand, it would probably mean higher overhead costs and a not inconsiderable disruption of
business. *con.*

(x)

Cause

In conclusion, we found that any change in the
physical environment, whether it was improved
lighting, the introduction of taped music, or new
decor, produced an increase in the employees' morale.
This in turn seemed to result in higher worker
effect productivity.

Content is the first consideration when choosing an organizer because sometimes the content will determine which organizer(s) can be used. For example, how would you organize the listings in the telephone book? a report on the costs of two intercom systems? instructions on using a fire extinguisher?

Libraries use several organizational systems for books—which ones are illustrated here?

If the content doesn't suggest a particular organizer, consider the purpose of your message. Although we can make some generalizations (for example, that simple listing, time order, and spatial order are usually used to describe or inform, and that pros and cons and comparison/contrast are usually used to persuade), there are no strict rules about each organizer being related to a specific purpose. For example, you may use pros and cons in a report to persuade your boss that the company should buy its own trucks for deliveries. Or you may use the same organizer simply to describe the various arguments for and against that option so that your boss can make a decision based on your information.

TAKE ACTION #3

A. Decide which pattern you would use to organize the following. As a class, discuss your decisions and your reasons for them. Remember that there is not necessarily only one correct answer for each situation.

(i) pictures of products on an advertising flyer

(ii) a report on the relationship between employee absenteeism and the weather

(iii) a brochure explaining the benefits and coverage of a company's insurance plan

(iv) an inventory of laboratory supplies

(v) a memo to your supervisor describing what can be cut from your department's budget and what must be kept

(vi) the basis for your decision on whether to accept or refuse a promotion which means transferring to a new branch office

(vii) the results of an investigation into several new sites for restaurant franchises

(viii) instructions for a new employee on balancing the money in the cash register at the end of each day

(ix) plans for the layout of a new warehouse

(x) a record of long-distance phone calls made by each department of a company

CHARTS AND GRAPHS

TAKE NOTE
Charts and graphs help you present (as the sender) or
understand (as the receiver) information more easily. They can
help simplify a lot of complex information, make a difficult
concept easier to grasp, emphasize certain points, and add
interest to a report or presentation.

Charts and graphs are often used to send a well-organized message
with high visual impact. They have always been popular in
business and industry as methods of relaying information but their
use has increased in recent years with the development of
computer graphics.

Charts and graphs are actually visual representations of some of
the organizers listed on p. 40. And, as with other messages, the
organizer you choose is determined by both the content and
purpose of your message.

For example, a flow chart is based on time order. Figure 2.1
shows the steps involved in a computer program which will drill
students in arithmetic problems. The chart of sales figures for two
years broken down by division and sales quarters uses comparison/
contrast and allows you to make comparisons in different categories
(see figure 2.2).

General to specific is used in the chart which shows the
responsibilities of various departments in a company (see figure
2.3). A chart which shows the hierarchy or line of command of a
company would be similar to the organization pattern of order of
importance or, in this case, order of authority (see figure 2.4).

Charts are, in general, descriptive. Graphs are quantitative; that
is, they illustrate things which can be measured. The bar graph in
figure 2.5 compares the favourite tasks of two groups of workers.
The circle graph (or pie graph) in figure 2.6 is also based on
comparison/contrast. It shows the percentage of a department's
total budget for each item.

An axis graph can show a measured quantity in relation to a
descriptive factor (see figure 2.7) or two measured qualities that are
related. The latter is sometimes used to illustrate cause and effect.
Figure 2.8 illustrates a relationship between sales and the amount
of money spent on advertising.

Figure 2.1

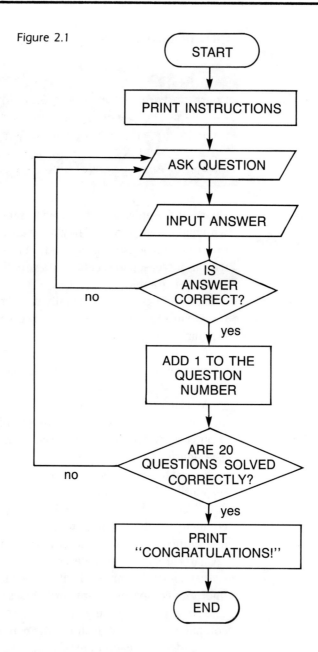

Figure 2.2

	This Year's Sales			Last Year's Sales		
	Div. A	Div. B	Total	Div. A	Div. B	Total
First Quarter	19067	15343	34410	18040	16821	34861
Second Quarter	25891	20462	46353	20561	19405	39966
Third Quarter	23823	17946	41769	21987	22161	44148
Fourth Quarter	20511	19723	40234	22167	15722	37889
Total	89292	73474	162766	82755	74109	156864

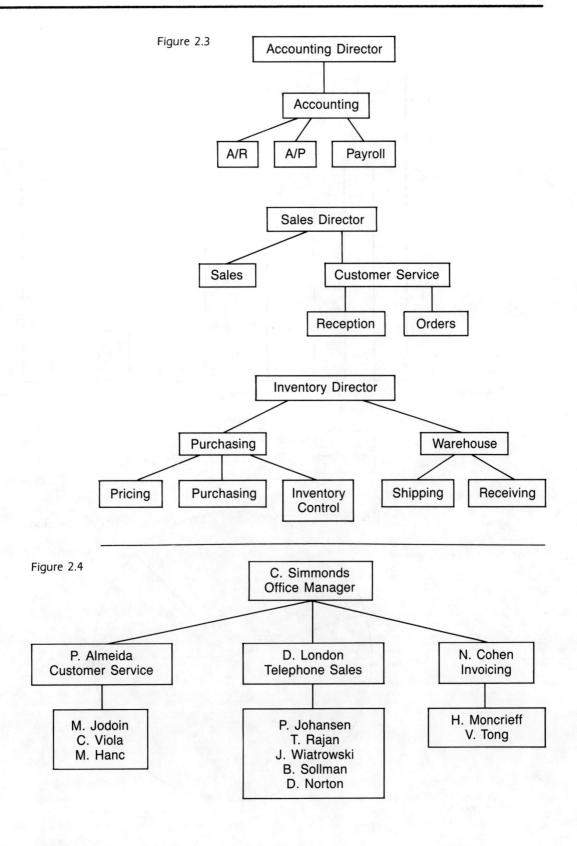

Figure 2.3

Figure 2.4

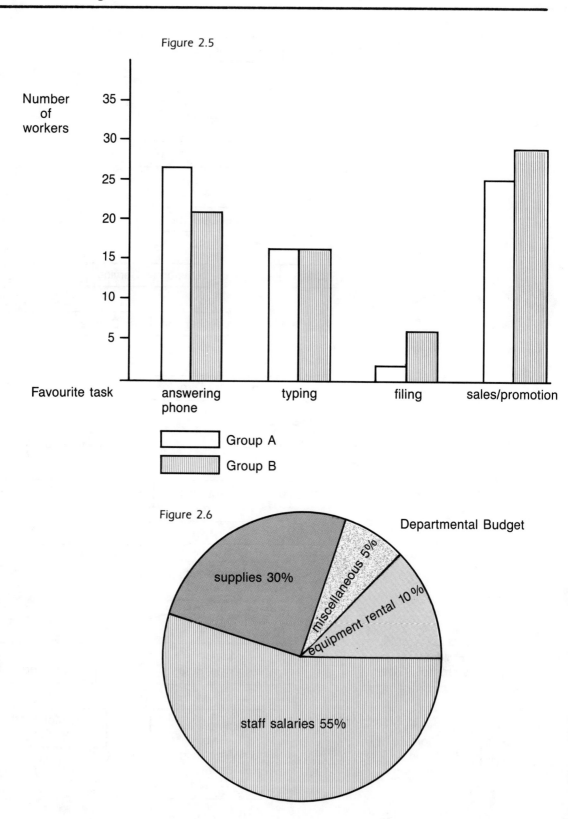

Figure 2.5

Number of workers

Favourite task

- answering phone
- typing
- filing
- sales/promotion

Group A
Group B

Figure 2.6

Departmental Budget

supplies 30%

miscellaneous 5%

equipment rental 10%

staff salaries 55%

Figure 2.7

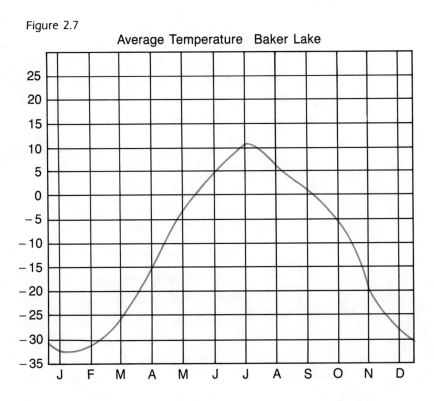

Average Temperature   Baker Lake

Figure 2.8

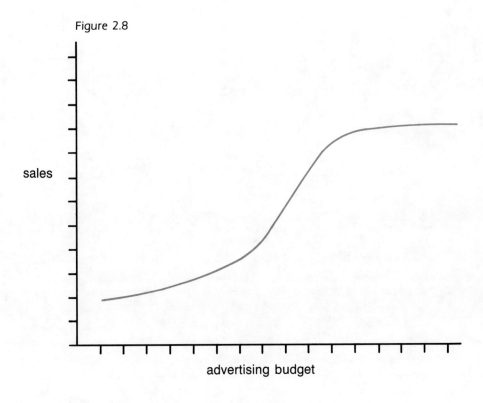

TAKE ACTION #4

A. Choose two of the following, gather the data necessary, then decide which type of chart or graph you would use to present the information. Write down your decisions and your reasons for them. Draw up the two charts or graphs and give them to your teacher for evaluation.

(i) Show the principal means of transportation to school of each person in the class.

(ii) Divide the students in your class into two groups based on a criterion such as age or gender and compare the favourite television shows of each group.

(iii) Describe how to do one of the tasks in your job.

(iv) Describe the average amount of time per week each student in your class spends listening to the radio.

(v) Describe the average number of people in your class who participate in outdoor sports each month of the year.

JOB SEARCH II

Getting Organized

JOB LEADS

You cannot treat your search for a job as a hit-or-miss activity. If you are looking for a full-time job, then you should be looking on a full-time basis — five days a week, eight hours a day. The greater the number of leads you develop and follow, the greater your chances of getting a job. You should plan each day of the week. For example, you could work from 8:00 a.m. to noon gathering leads and making telephone contacts. After lunch from 1:00 p.m. to 5:00 p.m. you could go for interviews, make personal contacts, or mail out résumés. Your first step is to purchase a daily diary and appointment book.

Most of the job leads you will develop will be classified as "hidden" leads. The term hidden is used because these positions are not advertised — you must hunt them out. Visible job leads include the help wanted ads and bulletin board notices. Contrary to popular belief, only 15 per cent of all possible job openings are visible leads. Because they are visible, the majority of job hunters go after them which creates fierce competition. Advertising positions takes time, money, and effort. Too often, there are too many unsuitable applications. Companies would rather wait for the first good job seeker to come in the door.

The following sources for job leads are in order from most effective to least effective. Do not limit yourself to one type of lead — use a variety of them to ensure that you have covered all possibilities.

CO-OPERATIVE EDUCATION, SCHOOL WORK EXPERIENCE

An important goal of these two school-based programs is to give students exposure to a company that might hire them. Supervisors at the placements used for these programs have had time to assess your abilities by seeing you in action. If a position is available and you have already proven yourself as a good worker, they will probably hire you instead of someone they do not know. In some cases, companies create new positions because they do not want to lose a good worker. If you like your placement, ask for an interview — don't assume that your supervisor will ask you. You can also ask about vacancies in other branches or departments of the placement.

FRIENDS AND RELATIVES

It is essential that you tell everyone you know that you are looking for a job. (Some companies have rules that relatives cannot work in the same place of business. However, your relatives can make inquiries on your behalf with their friends.)

HELP WANTED ADS

A help wanted ad will usually tell you:

- what kind of job is being advertised
- what skills you need in order to apply for that specific job
- whom to contact for an interview
- how to apply for an interview

If there is not enough information in the ad, you should ask for more when you call or write to apply for the job. (See p. 57 for more information about help wanted ads.)

PERSONAL ADS

You can write an ad that briefly outlines your qualifications and the type of job you are seeking. The ad can be placed in newspapers, in magazines, and on bulletin boards.

EMPLOYMENT AGENCIES

Government

The major centres are run by the Ministry of Employment and Immigration. After completing an application form, you will be interviewed by an employment counsellor. Your application is kept on file and you will be called if a suitable opening arises. There are also large boards displaying jobs available in your area. Often, special youth employment centres are set up either year-round or for summer jobs. Check your area centre to see what services are available. Many centres also provide courses on how to look for a job.

Private

Private employment agencies are set up to help both the job seeker and the companies who are looking for employees. The process you go through is similar to that for the employment centre. The agency will send you to a particular company for an interview if your qualifications match those required. Agencies should not charge you for this service since they are paid by the companies which hire them.

POSTED SIGNS

As well as bulletin boards in employment centres and your school there are often notices posted in shopping centres, community centres, and churches.

NEWS STORIES (Newspapers, television, radio)

If a new company is moving to your area there is often a news item about it. Don't wait—let them know you are available as soon as possible.

Some radio stations have a special program on job opportunities in their area. Listen!

YELLOW PAGES, BUSINESS DIRECTORIES, TRADE MAGAZINES

These are good sources of information about what companies are in your area. They are available at your library.

CHAMBERS OF COMMERCE, BUSINESS AND TRADE ORGANIZATIONS

Use the Yellow Pages to find out which of the above exist in your community. These groups can provide you with lists of companies in your chosen field. You can also ask for advice on how to find employment.

SCHOOL GUIDANCE DEPARTMENTS AND PLACEMENT OFFICES

Companies may call your school asking the guidance counsellors for students who are interested in working for them. Tell your counsellor what type of job you are seeking. Some schools set up a bulletin board. Check the board daily.

CONTENTS OF HELP WANTED ADS

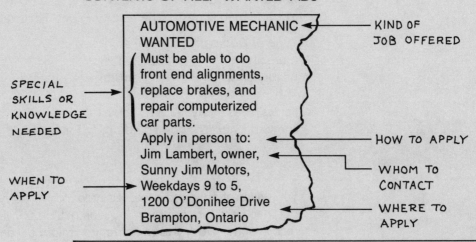

AUTOMOTIVE MECHANIC WANTED ◄—— KIND OF JOB OFFERED

SPECIAL SKILLS OR KNOWLEDGE NEEDED ——► Must be able to do front end alignments, replace brakes, and repair computerized car parts.

Apply in person to: ◄—— HOW TO APPLY

Jim Lambert, owner, ◄—— WHOM TO CONTACT

WHEN TO APPLY ——► Sunny Jim Motors, Weekdays 9 to 5, 1200 O'Donihee Drive Brampton, Ontario ◄—— WHERE TO APPLY

ABBREVIATIONS COMMONLY FOUND IN WANT ADS

The following words and their abbreviations are often found in help wanted ads.

appt.	appointment	loc.	located, location
asst.	assistant	mach.	machine
avail.	available	mfg.	manufacturing
bldg.	building	mfr.	manufacturer
bus.	business	min.	minimum
co.	company	mo.	month
cond.	conditions	nec.	necessary
dept.	department	op.	operator
exc.	excellent	pd.	paid
exp.	experience(d)	p/t	part-time
ext.	extension	ref.	references
gen.	general	rep.	representative
hr.	hour, hours	secy.	secretary
hrly.	hourly	temp.	temporary
H.S.	High School	vac.	vacation
grad.	graduate	wk.	week
immed.	immediately	wpm	words per minute
incl.	including	yr.	year

GETTING DOWN TO BUSINESS #1

A. Make a list of the people you know who work in jobs or companies that interest you. This list can include neighbours and parents of friends as well as your own friends and relatives.

B. (i) List the types of companies you might want to work for and then decide what headings you would use to look them up in trade magazines or the Yellow Pages. For example:

Type of Company	Headings
plumbing	Plumbers
beauty shop	Hairdressers, Beauticians

(ii) Using as many leads as you can, create a list of up to ten companies where you could apply for a job.

You will probably find it necessary to follow many of the leads outlined here for your own job search. Unless you keep a record of the work you're doing, you might become so disorganized that you miss opportunities.

GETTING DOWN TO BUSINESS #2

A. As a class make up a chart to help you organize your job search. Include space for such information as the name, address, and phone number of each company and the person you contacted, when and how you inquired about a job and what the response was, and any necessary follow-up action. Make a copy of this chart for your own use and keep it in your Job Search Kit.

THE BUSINESS OF READING

3

Reading is to the mind what exercise is to the body.
SIR RICHARD STEELE

TAKE NOTE
In any career you spend a great deal of time reading: letters, memos, advertisements, instructions, reports, technical manuals, newspapers, trade magazines, and books. In your private life, too, reading brings you both information and entertainment. Good reading skills are essential for effective communication.

BIZARRO   By DAN PIRARO

Reginald relaxes at home
with a few good books.

TAKE ACTION #1

A. Think of some of the written messages you have received in the past week. Your teacher will give you a chart like the one shown below. Fill in the blanks for five messages. As a class, discuss your choices.

Sender	Receiver	Message	Format of message
Ministry of Transportion	me as a driver	stop	sign post
Dan Piraro	me reading the Globe and Mail	Reginald relaxes at home with a few good books.	cartoon
cereal company	me at breakfast	Wheat Gems put a sparkle in your day.	cereal box
my brother	me, reading a note on the refrigerator	Remember to feed the cats before you go to bed.	note

READING RATE

Throughout life we are continually bombarded with things to read. As an efficient employee, you must pick out the important messages and discard or give limited attention to the less important ones. To do this you must learn to identify very quickly the purpose of each written communication. One way of doing this is to skim-read each message as you receive it. Complex or important messages will require further study.

Your reading rate will change according to the importance of the message, the level of language, and the complexity of the material. You can **skim-read** a message when the words are familiar (the language is colloquial or informal) and when you are not concerned with remembering every detail. Skim-reading involves moving your eyes quickly over written material, searching out the most essential facts. You skim-read advertisements in newspapers and magazines, boring parts of novels, and chapters of nonfiction books that contain very little information that you require.

You will have to **read with concentration** whenever the information presented in the message is important to you, such as when you are studying for a test or when you are reading instructions on how to operate new office equipment or home appliances. When you are reading to retain almost every detail, your eye movements slow down, you may mentally rephrase the ideas presented in your own words, and you may even take notes in order to remember the material better. If words that you don't know are used in a passage take time to look them up in a dictionary.

Proofreading
The rate at which you read material you are proofreading will be even slower than that at which you read with concentration. When proofreading you are, of course, concentrating, but you are not simply concentrating to *understand*; you are also *examining* the material to ensure it is correct (see chapter 5, "The Business of Writing," p. 105).

© Jefferson Communications, Inc. 1985
Distributed by Tribune Media Services, Inc.

TAKE ACTION #2

A. Bring to class two examples of written messages you would skim-read and two examples of written messages you would have to read with concentration. As a class, discuss why each message belongs in either the "skim" or "concentrate" category. Remember to consider:

- importance of the information to you
- language level
- complexity of the message

PURPOSE

> TAKE NOTE
> When you understand the sender's purpose, you are better able to judge the value or importance of the message.

You must be able to detect the difference between information which is intended to influence your emotions or attitudes and straightforward, factual information.

Propaganda, for example, is written in a style which reflects the author's purpose to persuade, while straightforward information is written in a matter-of-fact style, reflecting the writer's purpose to inform (leaving you to decide a course of action or an opinion for yourself). Other purposes include entertainment, instruction, praise, and criticism. What others can you think of?

TAKE ACTION #3

A. Read each of the following passages. As a class, discuss what you think the writer's purpose is in each case.

(i) Fewer people would get sick if hobbies were more often investigated as potential causes of ailments and illness. The Health and Welfare committee is working to encourage health practitioners to consider art supplies as possible causes when their patients turn up with everything from persistent sniffles to chronic bronchial trouble, even cancer. (53)
From *Canadian Consumer* (January 1986)

(ii) Anne broke into a run as she hurried towards her afterschool job at Ogden's department store. It made no difference that she was the boss's daughter; Mrs. Turner would have her head if she was five minutes late!

Dad was out of town anyway. A sense of adventure glowed somewhere in Anne's mid-section as she reminded herself that both Mom and Dad would be away for two whole weeks . . . It was such a glorious feeling of freedom. (70)
From *Anne and Jay*, Barbara Bartholomew

(iii) The operating environment may affect copier performance. Avoid the following conditions:
- extreme temperatures
- areas where dust accumulates
- direct sunlight (19)

(iv) Agnes Rutherford is a fine upstanding member of our community who would be an excellent member of Parliament. No one has done more for this area than she has in the last five years. Ms. Rutherford is highly educated, keenly motivated and sincerely devoted to your concerns. A vote for Agnes Rutherford is a vote for superior representation in Ottawa.

(v) In independent houshold tests TOPS beat out other floor cleaners. But that's hardly surprising—they can't cut through grime or leave a shine like TOPS. Make your floor TOPS.

(vi) Although our product has been on the market for only two months, we believe you will want your company to be our local distributor. Your success is guaranteed. All your customers will be asking you for Hot 'n' Spicy Hamburger Sauce. Brand recognition has become almost universal. Surely you don't want a competing distributor to be selling such a high-demand item.

CONTENT

The content of a message is the information being sent.
In order to understand this you must be able to pick out the main
idea and all the important facts and arguments related to it.

TAKE ACTION #4

A. Read the following passage and identify:

(i) the main idea presented

(ii) four other facts or ideas related to that idea

PERCEPTION OF STRESS KEY TO HANDLING IT PSYCHOLOGIST SAYS

WINNIPEG (CP) — Despite opening night jitters and bouts of
unemployment between plays, actress Maggie Nagle loves her job
and has rarely thought about leaving the stage for a more secure
occupation.

Shirley Harder also won't give up her job as a telephone opera-
tor, though it's one filled with a constant bombardment of calls
and the threat of being replaced by a machine.

Harder and Nagle, both 26, have one thing in common—stressful jobs they won't readily give up. However, they differ in one major respect: their perception of their jobs and the degree of control they have over them.

It's these two factors that are seen by stress experts as fundamental to determining how much pressure people face at work.

"It's not the job, but how a person perceives it—that's what's crucial," says John Arnett, a psychologist at the University of Manitoba's faculty of medicine.

Lissa Donner, executive director of the Occupational Health Centre of the Manitoba Federation of Labor, says stress levels are also based on the amount of control an employee has in the workplace measured against the demands placed on the worker.

But for Harder, there's no control. When an early fall snowstorm hit Winnipeg recently she faced an extra barrage of calls at work.

"We have no way of controlling the calls that come in," says Harder, who handles an average of 1000 calls a day on a typical seven-hour shift.

"You get a lot of people on tranquillizers, Valium, anti-depressants," Harder says.

Nagle says that while she too finds her job stressful, she loves what she does.

"You're incredibly nervous," she says of opening nights. "You're pumped up. It's World Series time and there's a lot riding on it.

"The performing life is a roller coaster, up and down. You need both. You can't sustain being up all the time."

From *The Toronto Star* (November 13, 1985)

B. Re-read the passage to determine which organizer was used by the writer.

Did it help your understanding of the main idea? Could any other organizer have been used to get the message across as effectively?

READING THE NEWSPAPER

The previous passage was taken from a daily newspaper.
Reading a good daily paper will help your knowledge of business and industry. Most newspapers have a business section that contains information on every aspect of professional life.

TAKE ACTION #5

A. Find an article dealing with a work-related topic in your daily newspaper (for example, safety on the job or the growth of small business). Bring your article to class and explain to the class why you chose it as a good example of informative business communication.

B. Submit the article to your teacher along with a brief outline of:

  (i) the main idea presented

  (ii) two or three supporting facts that were used to develop the main idea

  (iii) any organizer used by the writer in an effective way

  (iv) the identity of the writer (if possible)

  (v) the writer's purpose in composing the article

C. Make a collage on a classroom bulletin board of the best articles brought in. Be on the alert for newspaper articles which present material of interest to you and continue to add to this collage over the next few months.

READING PROFESSIONAL AND TRADE MAGAZINES

Another way to learn about particular careers and professions is to read trade or professional magazines. These magazines specialize in professional areas such as plumbing, secretarial science, hairdressing, accounting, commercial art, and so on.

Trade and professional magazines are good sources for possible job leads as well as for information about new developments in the fields they cover.

TAKE ACTION #6

A. Find a copy of a trade or professional magazine that reflects the interests and concerns in the field you wish to enter. You might ask a business, technical, or family studies teacher for a recommendation. Your school or public librarian will also help you locate the most appropriate magazine by using either *The Canadian Periodical Index* (Ottawa: Canadian Library Association) or *Business Periodical Index* (New York: H. W. Wilson).

B. Fill in a copy of the profile for trade and professional magazines (pp. 70-71) which will be given to you by your teacher.

TRADE AND PROFESSIONAL MAGAZINE PROFILE

Name of magazine _____

Publisher's name _____

address _____

_____

Special fields for which the magazine is published

_____

Circulation (How many people read the magazine?)

_____

How would you most likely obtain a copy of this magazine?

(a) on a news-stand_____

(b) at your place of business_____

(c) by purchasing a subscription_____

(d) at a library_____

Scan the magazine's table of contents and list three or four articles which sound as if they might be useful to you.

_____

_____

_____

_____

_____

Decide which article on the list interests you the most.

After you read it answer the following questions:

(a) What was the article about? _____

_____

_____

(b) Briefly, what did you learn? _____

_____

_____

(c) Identify one organizer that the writer used. Was it effective? Why or why not?

_____

_____

_____

_____

_____

(d) Do you agree or disagree with the writer's main ideas? Explain why.

_____

_____

_____

_____

If you were currently working in the trade or business for which your magazine is written, how could you benefit from reading this magazine regularly?

_____

_____

_____

Who would benefit most from reading this magazine (employee in business or trade, or owner/manager of business or trade?)

_____

_____

_____

_____

TAKE ACTION #7

A. Examine the following selections from trade and professional magazines.

(i) SPEEDING THE PACE

The electronic world of the automated office is drawing nearer. Taking full advantage of it, however, does not so automatically arrive. It requires planning, coordination, and cooperation — and some willingness to compromise and experience the pain of changing toward a common environment before the benefits of a seamless environment, with every piece of text and information available to every user, arrives. A little planning and extra thought in the early stages of front office computer usage can go a very long way toward avoiding pain and the distress of temporary (and seemingly endless) incompatibility in later stages. And a little willingness to be flexible and to consider the needs of the overall organization—rather than just optimizing for local needs—will go a long way in speeding up the pace at which the benefits of the electronic office can be enjoyed.

From "WP Software: the status of compatibility", Amy Wohl, *Office Equipment & Methods* (Jan./Feb. 1986)

(ii)

(iii) BELL LABS BRINGS FIBER–OPTIC PHONES CLOSER TO HOME

Telephone companies have long dreamed of extending their fiber-optic systems all the way into the home, making the phone network the keystone of tomorrow's information society, with more than enough capacity for video, text, and audio signals. That futuristic vision has been dampened by economic realities: the staggering cost of installing a laser in every home to generate the pulses of light that carry outgoing conversations and computer messages. But last month, AT&T Bell Laboratories unveiled a technique that promises to make fiber-optic telephones practical.

The trick is done with mirrors. In place of a home laser, a tiny mirror in the photodetector in home phones reflects laser light piped in from the phone company's switching station. The reflected beam of light is then modulated to represent the caller's voice or carry digital data as it bounces back to the switching station. The concept has been demonstrated over an optical-fiber link more than a mile long.

From "Developments to Watch", *Business Week* (March 17, 1986)

(iv)

B. For each excerpt:

(i) outline the message.

(ii) explain the sender's purpose.

(iii) explain what techniques the sender uses to accomplish the purpose.

People read for both information and pleasure—approximately 16 per cent of our communication is reading.

C. Compare the selections and outline the similarities and differences in their purposes and messages.

HELPFUL READING TOOLS

Table of Contents

When you are looking for specific information in a book or magazine, the table of contents will direct you to the exact chapter or
page containing the information you are seeking. A table of contents will provide you with a list of chapter headings and in some
cases, sub-headings and the corresponding page numbers. In some
books the table of contents is followed by a list of illustrations,
charts, or tables, which will also be of help to you when you're
looking for specific information.

Index

The index appears at the back of the book and gives you the exact
page on which material about specific topics, people, or companies
appears.

Introduction

Sometimes when you search in a book for a particular piece of
information you might decide to read the entire book. You can
usually get the flavour of a publication by reading either the
introduction or the first chapter.

TAKE ACTION #8

A. Read the following two passages, which are taken from the introduction to a well-known business book, *In Search of Excellence: Lessons from America's Best-Run Companies*, by Thomas J. Peters and Robert H. Waterman, Jr.

We had decided, after dinner, to spend a second night in Washington. Our business day had taken us beyond the last convenient flight out. We had no hotel reservations, but were near the new Four Seasons, had stayed there once before, and liked it. As we walked through the lobby wondering how best to plead our case for a room, we braced for the usual chilly shoulder accorded to late-comers. To our astonishment, the concierge looked up, smiled, called us by name, and asked how we were. She remembered our names! We knew in a flash why in the space of a brief year the Four Seasons had become the "place to stay" in the District and was a rare first-year holder of the venerated four-star rating.

Good for them, you are thinking, but why the big deal? Well, the incident hit us with some force because for the past several years we have been studying corporate excellence. For us, one of the main clues to corporate excellence has come to be just such incidents of unusual effort on the part of apparently ordinary employees. When we found not one but a host of such incidents, we were pretty certain we were on the track of an exceptional situation. What's more, we were fairly sure we would find sustained financial performance that was as exceptional as the employees' performance.

●　　●　　●

Wherever we have been in the world, from Australia to Europe to Japan, we can't help but be impressed by the high standard of cleanliness and consistency of service we find in every McDonald's hamburger outlet. Not everyone likes the product, nor the concept of McDonald's as a worldwide expression of American culture, but it really *is* extraordinary to find the kind of quality assurance McDonald's has achieved worldwide in a service business. (Controlling quality in a service business is a particularly difficult problem. Unlike manufacturing, in which one can sample what comes off the line and reject bad lots, what gets produced in service businesses and what gets consumed happens at the same time and in the same place. One must ensure that tens of thousands of people throughout the company are adhering roughly to the same high standard and that they all understand the company's conception of and genuine concern for quality.)

(360)

B. As a class, discuss the following:

(i) Do these two brief excerpts give you an idea of what the book is going to be like?

(ii) Would you like to read the entire book? Explain your answer.

C. Your teacher will give you a copy of the following reading checklist. Keep it handy as a reference to help you achieve effective reading skills.

READING CHECKLIST

When you read, you should:

☐ skim the material you are about to read quickly to gain an impression of the organization of the material (note the use of headings) and an understanding of the key points made or ideas presented.
☐ adapt your reading speed to the importance of the material being read.
☐ try to determine the meaning of an unfamiliar word by considering the context in which it is used.
☐ use a dictionary if you are in any doubt about a word's meaning.
☐ clarify your understanding of the material by mentally rephrasing the sender's statements in your own words.
☐ make notes that summarize key points if the material is particularly detailed and important.

THE BUSINESS OF LISTENING

4

It is the province of
knowledge to speak and it is
the privilege of wisdom to
listen.
OLIVER WENDELL HOLMES

TAKE NOTE

You hear with your ears. You listen with your ears, your mind, and, often, your eyes. Listening is more than just hearing. Listening is understanding what you hear, evaluating it, and then reacting or responding to it. Hearing is a passive activity; listening is an active one.

Hearing is passive—you simply sense sounds. Listening is active—you must work at it. Try this experiment. Without stopping to think about it, write down on a piece of paper all the sounds you can hear coming from outside your classroom. Your teacher will give you fifteen seconds to do this. Now close your eyes and listen hard for sixty seconds (your teacher will tell you when time is up). Make a list of the sounds you heard and compare your two lists. Which list shows you were listening to the sounds, not just hearing them?

TAKE ACTION #1

A. Read through the following situations and decide which involve listening and which involve hearing. As a class, discuss your decisions and your reasons for them.

(i) During the morning school announcements you and your fellow students are talking about last night's television programs. Suddenly you realize that your name has just been announced but you don't know why.

(ii) You are in your room at home. The radio is turned up high and your favourite song is playing. Without knocking, your younger brother and sister come in, eager to discuss plans for the three of you to go camping next summer. You turn off the radio and focus your attention on them.

(iii) At breakfast one Saturday morning your mother is describing a shopping trip she's planning for that afternoon. You are absorbed in the entertainment section of the newspaper until she mentions looking for a new sweater for you.

(iv) The paper you wrote for your math test is returned to you marked 45 per cent. You ask your teacher to explain each problem to you after school that day. The teacher begins the conversation with: "I went over all the problems in class the day before the test . . ."

(v) Over the past few weeks you have been late for your part-time job on several occasions. You've always had an excuse but never a good one. Your boss calls you aside to talk about the importance of getting to work on time. You decide to treat the whole embarrassing situation as if it were a huge joke.

You always have a reason for listening. Usually you listen for information, instructions, or pleasure. In diagram form that would look like this:

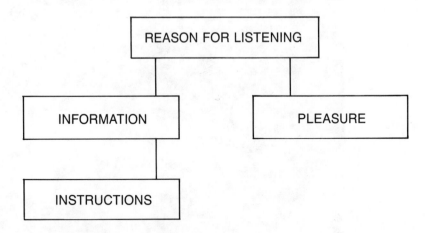

• Why do you think listening for information and listening for instructions are linked?
• In a business situation which reason(s) for listening will occur most often?

LISTENING SKILLS

TAKE NOTE
A good listener is someone who:
  • concentrates on what is being said.
  • has an open-minded attitude.
  • works to understand the message which is being sent.

Poor concentration, a non-receptive attitude, and lack of understanding are all barriers to effective listening. Working to overcome these barriers will help you:
  • be more observant and alert.
  • follow instructions and perform tasks better.
  • learn to accept helpful criticism.
  • be more open-minded about yourself and others.
  • improve your ability to communicate and get along with others.

It's important to strengthen listening skills—approximately 45 per cent of our communication is spent listening. What good listening habits are being practised here? Are there any obvious barriers to communication?

TAKE ACTION #2

A. Use copies of the checklists below and on p. 86, to evaluate your listening skills. As you read the checklists, make a note of any areas where you feel you need improvement. Working with a partner, discuss ways in which each of you could strengthen your listening skills.

LISTENING CHECKLIST — Concentration

When you listen, you should:

☐ pay attention to the speaker, not allowing other noises to distract you.
☐ listen carefully and take notes if necessary.
☐ change the physical set-up if necessary; for example, move to a better seat, turn off noisy machinery.
☐ understand the purpose and become involved in what is being said.
☐ try not to think about personal problems.
☐ make sure you don't daydream. (The difference between the rate of thinking [500 words a minute] and the rate of speaking [125 words a minute] enables a good listener to spend that extra time evaluating what the speaker is saying. Don't fill in the time by daydreaming.)

Background noise can be a barrier to good listening. How would you solve the problem shown here?

Translators for the hearing impaired take advantage of the fact that our rate of listening is higher than our rate of speaking. They must listen to what is being said, while translating what they have just heard.

LISTENING CHECKLIST — Attitude

When you listen, you should:

☐ listen without letting your prejudices or emotions get in the way.

☐ hear what is really said, not what you want to hear or expect the speaker to say.

☐ pay attention even if the speaker's vocabulary, physical appearance, or mannerisms are distracting.

☐ try not to jump to conclusions.

LISTENING CHECKLIST — Understanding

When you listen, you should:

☐ consciously work at understanding what you hear.

☐ use a dictionary. (A large vocabulary helps contribute to good listening skills. Record words you don't understand and look them up.)

☐ ask for help when you do not understand something.

☐ use the company manual to study words used on the job.

B. (i) Working in groups of two or three, choose one of the situations from Take Action #1 (p. 82). Discuss the situation thoroughly in your group, then write a draft of the conversation. As you are working make sure that you are able to identify:

- the sender, receiver, and message in your example
- any barriers to effective communication your example illustrates
- ways in which these barriers can be overcome

(ii) Demonstrate your situation to the rest of the class. As each group makes its presentation, work on your own to take brief notes which answer the following questions:

- What is the message? Who are the sender and receiver?
- What are the communication barriers?
- How does the group deal with them?

(iii) After all the groups have completed their presentations, discuss each of the five situations as a class. Refer to the notes you made during the individual presentations and try to reach a class consensus on the questions you answered.

USING FEEDBACK

TAKE NOTE
The receiver of a message uses feedback to help clarify the message. Feedback can be oral, written, and non-verbal (body language, facial expressions, etc.) Feedback makes the listening process easier by helping the receiver to understand the message.

TAKE ACTION #3
A. Work with a partner and role-play this business telephone situation.

Receptionist: Smith and Jones Company Limited.
Caller: Smithers Stone Company?
Receptionist: No. Smith and Jones. Go ahead, please. (Other lines are lighting up; someone enters the office.)
Caller: Could you please tell Mr. Abe Brown that I am unable to make our original appointment and that he can meet me, Mrs. Cyle, at noon on Friday in my office?
Receptionist: Fine, thank you.

(Time lapses and the receptionist sees Mr. Green and gives him the message to meet Mrs. Cyle at noon on Friday in his office.)

(ii) Consider the following questions and discuss your answers with your partner:

- What listening errors are made during this conversation?
- What are the results for Mrs. Cyle, Mr. Green, and Mr. Brown?
- How could using feedback remedy this situation?

(iii) Changing roles with your partner occasionally, experiment with different ways of solving the communication problems here. Write out the best solution, then discuss your ideas as a class.

TAKING NOTES

One form of written feedback is taking notes while listening. A note made during a telephone conversation, informal meeting, or lecture enhances good listening skills by helping you to understand the message. Refer to the checklist on p. 89 for tips to help you achieve effective notetaking skills.

LISTENING CHECKLIST — Notetaking

When you take notes, you should:

☐ use forms when available.
☐ write neatly and identify notes with date, topic, and speaker.
☐ write down the main ideas, supporting ideas, and facts. Do not try to write everything. Be selective!
☐ make additional notes in the margin—such as questions you might wish to ask for clarification.
☐ listen for clues that warn you an important point is about to be made.
☐ write notes in your own words, using point form.
☐ review your notes and, if necessary, summarize them in order to condense them and put them in logical order. It may help if you put them in sentence form.
☐ review your notes for new vocabulary. Make a list of new words and look them up in the dictionary.

The ability to take good notes helps you:

- extend your memory.
- organize your thoughts.
- gather information.
- learn new material.
- review old material.
- summarize.

FORMS

Forms are an important business tool. They assist you by making it easier to record vital information while listening. Using forms also means there is information you don't have to write down.

TAKE ACTION #4

A. With a partner, take turns reading the following messages and taking down the facts. Decide what type of forms could be used in each situation. Remember to use verbal feedback if necessary.

(i) Would you please send me information on your new product, So-White? My address is 1880 Eglinton Avenue East, Level 3, Toronto, Ontario M1P 3D0.

(ii) I would like to order the Number 1 special without the fries but with the spinach salad. Please give me my tea after my meal. Oh, and I will also have a glass of water now.

(iii) I am the parts manager of TSR systems. I want 5000 units of the 5 cm pipe; 10 000 brass screws, size two; and 50 brass fittings. Please phone me at 1-403-555-9090 if this will have to go on backorder.

B. Your teacher will give you some telephone message forms and then read some messages to you. Take down the necessary information as each message is read. As a class, discuss what information should have been recorded in each situation.

TAKE ACTION ON THE JOB #1

A. (i) Which forms are used in your company? With your supervisor's permission collect samples of all the forms that you and/or your co-workers use when taking down information over the phone. Ask your co-workers if using the form makes their job easier and why.

(ii) Set up a class display of all the forms which were brought in.

LISTENING FOR CLUES

Often a speaker gives you clues that something important is about to be said. These clues are words that lead into an important point. "The next point is," "on the other hand," "an example is," and "in conclusion" are examples of clues. Always listen for clues and make note of the points that follow them.

TAKE ACTION #5

A. Choose someone in the class to read this lecture. Make notes during it. During the lecture, think of one question you would like to ask at its conclusion.

"There are many behaviours that disrupt the workplace. In a recent survey it was shown that dishonesty and lying topped the list. If a company believes that an employee lacks integrity, all positive qualities become meaningless. The other deadly sins are known to all of us to some degree.

"After dishonesty, the next most annoying behaviour is irresponsibility — goofing off and doing personal business on company time.

"Following irresponsibility is arrogance. An example of this would be employees who spend more time boasting about their accomplishments than on actually getting the job done. Fourth on the list are absenteeism and lateness. The two go hand in hand.

"The remaining irritations are not following instructions or ignoring company policies, whining and complaining, and last on the list was laziness and lack of motivation.

"In conclusion, I wish to stress that incorrect personal behaviour is a cause for dismissal in 85 per cent of all firings. Firings are not, and I stress not, skill related."

B. Read the lecture silently to yourself and list the clues contained in it. Compare this list with the notes you made, to see if you identified all the clues and the important points that followed.

C. Prepare a formal summary (with title) of this lecture from your notes and give it to your teacher for evaluation.

A good listener is able to pick out the important points and make decisions while listening.

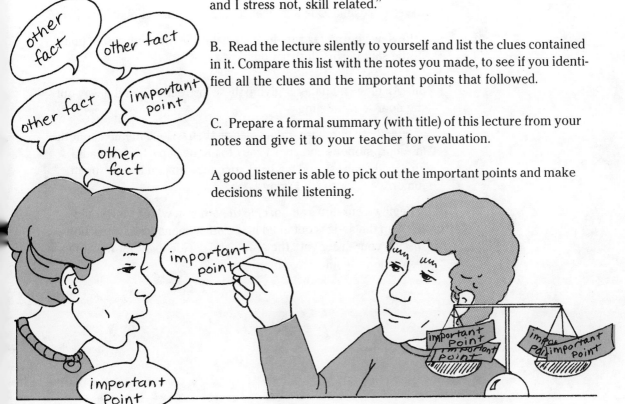

TAKE ACTION #6

A. Work in groups of three and have each member of your group read one of the following situations aloud to the other two. As you listen, make notes to remind yourself of the important points of each situation.

(i) A co-worker is telling you about a situation in another department:

"Two people were hired at the same time for the same kind of work. Sam was very fast, highly organized, and accurate. Angela did her work and got along well with her co-workers but was not the perfectionist Sam was. Sam was absent often. Angela was always on the job. When there was less business and a layoff was inevitable, everyone thought Angela would go but it was Sam they let go."

Review your notes and decide as a group the business practice that is emphasized in this situation.

(ii) A plant supervisor is talking to a worker:

"This work area is looking pretty messy. These empty cartons and scrap pieces of wood lying around could cause an accident. We haven't had an accident in over six months. Take care of it, will you?"

Review your notes and decide what is the most important point in the supervisor's instructions.

(iii) An office manager is giving these instructions on the way out the door to a meeting.

"File these purchase orders please, then write a memo about the latest promotions and give a copy to all the department heads. First, call Shairose and tell her I am unable to join her for lunch tomorrow. Ask her if Friday is okay."

Review your notes and decide the order in which you would perform the duties contained in the office manager's instructions. Discuss your order with the group and decide together how the instructions should have been given.

B. Your teacher will read a passage from the newspaper. Make notes while you are listening. Write down just enough to keep a record of the most important points. When you are finished, your teacher will list the important points. Compare your work with the teacher's list.

C. Your teacher has prepared a tape approximately three minutes long which presents the closing portion of a lecture or speech. Make notes to record the key ideas presented in these concluding remarks. Edit your notes and prepare a final copy to give to your teacher for evaluation.

D. Work in your small groups. Have each member of your group read aloud one of the following paragraphs from a training seminar. As you listen, take notes. After each person is finished, summarize the paragraph in two sentences. Compare your summaries, then hand them in to your teacher for evaluation.

(i) "A rumour is a message generally based on gossip not facts. It is wise to think twice before responding to a rumour. There may be several reasons rumours occur — mischief-making, insecurity among employees, or boredom. On the other hand, rumours sometimes develop because people are rushed, are too busy, or simply do not get the message straight."

(ii) "Busy people seem to attract more responsibilities and more new things to do. Be sure to keep yourself active and busy, even if you have to push yourself hard to do it. If you keep on the move you will be involved and you will continue to learn. The moment you become bored, look around for something to do."

(iii) "Almost every day workers are faced with problems that need solving. One way to solve problems is to report every one to your supervisor and follow the instructions you receive. People with initiative, however, try to come up with solutions themselves, before taking the issue to the supervisor."

LOOKING FOR CLUES

TAKE NOTE
Often, it is easier to understand the message being sent when you can see, as well as hear, the speaker.

TAKE ACTION #7
A. Your teacher will show a videotape of an interview show or business report program seen on television. (See copyright notice on p. ix .) First the teacher will play only the audio part of the tape for the class. While you listen, make notes that record the most important ideas you hear. Then your teacher will play the same tape again, using both audio and video. Again take notes recording the most important ideas. As a class, discuss when more information was recorded and why. By looking at parts of the videotape again, identify the particular body language and facial expressions of the speakers which might have helped you to record a more detailed impression of what was said.

B. Your teacher will divide the class into groups of three or four. Each group will prepare a videotaped or live presentation to be shown eventually to the entire class.

(i) Begin by preparing a shooting script on one of the following business situations:

—The receptionist of your company must deal with an angry customer who storms into the office to complain about an important order that has been filled incorrectly. Your cast should include at least one other employee of the company, as well as the receptionist and the customer. Your script should illustrate some barrier to communication that is overcome by one member of your cast.

—The boss is leaving for a three-day conference and wants to give a member of his staff instructions about what to do while he is away. Someone else in the office keeps interrupting this important conversation. Your script should show how the boss overcomes this barrier to communication effectively. It should also show how the staff member makes sure the instructions will be remembered and acted upon.

—Two employees of a small company are arguing because each wants to take vacation time in the same weeks of July. One employee is nasty and belligerent; the other is more calm and logical. When the boss comes in, show that the calm, cool, and collected employee is more likely to get what she/he wants.

—Any other business situation approved by your teacher that demonstrates a problem in office communication (specifically, overcoming a listening problem).

(ii) Once you have written a script that clearly defines and presents your chosen situation, decide on the cast and practise the parts of your skit.

(iii) Shoot the script with the help of your teacher, the audio-visual technician, and/or the mass media teacher in your school, if these resources are available; if they are not, present a live performance of your situation for your class.

(iv) Each group will present its videotape and the teacher and the entire class will evaluate each presentation using a copy of the checklist on p. 96.

LISTENING PRESENTATION CHECKLIST

Rate each category on a scale from 1 (Needs Improvement) to 10 (Excellent)—a score of 6 would mean Satisfactory. Add up your ratings to find your total score.

IS THE PRESENTATION:

STRAIGHTFORWARD? (Is the dialogue easy to follow?)

1   2   3   4   5   6   7   8   9   10

Comments: _____

_____

CONTROLLED? (Are the actors taking their parts seriously?)

1   2   3   4   5   6   7   8   9   10

Comments: _____

_____

EFFECTIVE? (Does the situation seem realistic?)

1   2   3   4   5   6   7   8   9   10

Comments: _____

_____

HELPFUL? (Does it offer a solution to a listening or communication problem? Can you tell what one person did to improve the communication problem presented?)

1   2   3   4   5   6   7   8   9   10

Comments: _____

_____

Score: _____

1 –20 Needs Improvement
21–25 Satisfactory
26–35 Good
36–40 Excellent

THE
BUSINESS
OF
WRITING

5

Learn to write well, or not to
write at all.
JOHN DRYDEN

TAKE NOTE
Written communications are often better than verbal communications because:
- they are clearer and less likely to be misunderstood.
- they serve as an official record of exactly what the message said.
- they can be re-read as often as necessary.
- if the message is for more than one person, everyone receives exactly the same message.

MEMORANDUM

TO: All Students   DATE: 19__ 03 13
FROM: Judi Misener   COPY TO: The teacher
SUBJECT: Writing Memos

   The most common method for internal office communications is the inter-office memo. Usually a printed form with headings similar to those on this memo is used. You can inform employees about business activities such as new procedures, meetings, or promotions. Sometimes you will ask employees to take action.

   A memo is usually only two or three paragraphs long. The first paragraph outlines what the memo is about; the second paragraph gives details; and the final paragraph describes what action, if required, should be taken. It is not necessary to sign your name at the end. Simply write your initials.

   I will be asking you to write many memos. Follow this example and you should do well!

gm

TAKE NOTE
The format you choose for any business communication depends on the audience (who is going to receive your message) and the purpose (why you are sending the message).

....*a note from*

Judi Misener

Co-operative Education

Hello students!
Don't be too alarmed, not all business writing involves "heavy" thinking and hard work.
Handwritten notes like this one are often used to communicate with co-workers.
I use this one all the time. What would yours look like?

Judi

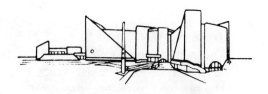

TAKE ACTION #1

A. For each of the following situations decide whether you would write a memo or a personal note. Discuss your decision and your reasons for it with a partner.

(i) You want to tell a co-worker that you can have lunch with her next Wednesday.

(ii) The staff must be informed of new work hours and holiday periods.

(iii) You wish to congratulate your friend and co-worker on winning the squash tournament at the local racquet club.

(iv) You wish to announce the member of the planning department who contributed the best suggestions for the month.

(v) You read an interesting article the members of the computer department might also find interesting.

(vi) The employees are to be informed about a change in timecard procedures.

B. As a class, discuss how you and your partner decided which situations required a memo and which required a personal note.

THE FOUR CS OF BUSINESS WRITING

In the following TAKE ACTION sections you will be asked to write some memos. When you are writing any business communication, ask yourself the following questions:

- **Is the message clear?**
Think about what you want to say and jot down your ideas on paper. Arrange the information in logical order.

- **Is the message concise?**
Say what you want to say in as few words as possible.

- **Is the message complete?**
Be certain all the essential information is given.

- **Is the message courteous?**
Showing consideration and good manners helps build a favourable company and personal image. A friendly, business-like tone builds goodwill between you and the receiver and gives the final polish to your work.

TAKE ACTION #2

A. In TAKE ACTION #1 you decided which situations required a memo and which ones deserved a personal note. Write the first paragraph only for the memos you would send. Compare your work with a partner's, then together write the best introductory paragraph for the first two memos.

B. Write the first and last paragraphs for the memos you would send in the following situations.

(i) You have decided that your employees need a change of routine. Next Tuesday you would like all employees to come to work dressed in a certain theme (of your choice). There will be a draw for a special prize (also of your choice).

(ii) New parking stickers will be issued to all employees next month. Each employee is to complete a form you will send with the memo. Employees are to return the form to the personnel department.

(iii) As chairperson of the Health and Safety Committee you wish to inform employees about a special lecture on stress management. They do not have to indicate ahead of time if they will be attending. The lecture is at 2:00 p.m. on Wednesday in Room 5.

C. Read this memo and in a memo to your teacher explain why it should be re-written.

TO: All Staff
FROM: I.M. Haggard
DATE: 19__ 03 17
SUBJECT: Punctuality

   The importance of punctuality in the business world cannot be over-emphasized enough. Punctuality shows an organized individual who has the right attitude that built this company to the sound financial position it is today. The starting time, as any good business person knows, is 8:30 a.m. I expect all employees to be on time or a penalty of docking pay will be put into effect.

   JmH.

(ii) Re-write the memo keeping in mind the four Cs—is the memo clear, concise, complete, and courteous?

D. In groups of three, choose two of the following situations. Using a printed form your teacher will give you, have each member of your group write a memo for both situations. Compare and discuss your work. Together write memos for the situations, using the best ideas and sentences from your individual memos.

(i) You have been attending school for many years now and have decided to inform the principal of a school rule you do not like. Write a memo to the principal outlining your concern and suggesting an alternative.

(ii) Write to your student council president concerning the same issue.

(iii) Develop a procedure that your class will use to deal with students who are late. Your memo will inform students of the new procedure.

(iv) You are working for a large firm that has a night-shift of its employees. The parking lot is not well lit and a car could be parked quite a distance from the entrance to the building. Safety for employees working the night-shift is a concern. A security guard is available to escort employees to their cars if they phone extension 7982.

(v) Proper business clothes are very important for the image of your company. You are to inform employees that wearing jeans, studded belts, or wrist bands, or having multi-coloured hair is not acceptable at the office.

TAKE ACTION ON THE JOB #1
A. If your job does not involve writing memos, speak to your supervisor and ask if you can be given the opportunity to do so. Ask permission, then make a copy of your work and bring it to class to be submitted in your writing folder. If you are already writing memos, ask your supervisor if you may bring in samples of your work to include in your folder.

THE FIFTH C OF BUSINESS WRITING
When you read each other's work did you notice spelling errors, misused words, or grammatical errors? There is a fifth C to remember.

Is the message correct?

Re-read your work several times. Check:

- spelling (use a dictionary)
- grammar (see Back to Basics, p. 249)
- correct meaning of words (If a word is new to you, look up the meaning in the dictionary to make sure you are using it correctly)
- typing errors (if you have a typed memo)
- missing words
- headings, initials, and names
- accuracy of math calculations

The increase in the volume and speed of communications made possible by today's technology places even more importance on accuracy.

Once again, ask yourself the first four Cs — is it clear, concise, complete, and courteous?

Proofreader's marks are standardized markings that you should use when correcting work. you can then re-type the work following the marks yourself you can give it to someone else to do. Proofreader's marks are shown in "Back to Basics" (p. 271).

The most powerful tool for making corrections is the word processor. At present, this new technology is used primarily by secretaries to correct other people's work. More time is saved if you write the original on a word processor and you make the corrections directly on it. Corrections such as changing words or adding new words, reorganizing sentences or paragraphs, and correcting spelling can be made in seconds. The result is a perfect copy without using two people's valuable time on one item. This time saving combined with a high speed printer can cut costs dramatically. A printer can produce an average of 150 letters a day.

Photocopiers that copy both sides, collate the pages, print different colours, and decrease or enlarge material have had a tremendous effect on the quality and quantity of written communications. The increased volume emphasizes the need for accuracy— one error can be duplicated 100 times in a matter of seconds. For your/own sake, check your work carefully.

BUSINESS LETTERS

TAKE NOTE
One well-written letter can produce thousands of dollars worth of business. It can also result in a repeat customer who will continue to generate business for your company. One poorly written letter can lose the same amount. To attract that lost customer to your company on another occasion could involve many additional hours of work and a great deal of company money.

YOUR ADDRESS

123 Ryan Road,
Medley, Alberta
TOA 2MO

DATE   19   05 10

All Business English Students,
Hometown High School,
456 Mark Street,
Quebec City, Quebec
G1P 2Q7

RECEIVER'S ADDRESS

Dear Students:

Have you ever wanted to complain to the manufacturer about a product you purchased? Is there a political issue you'd like to write about to your member of Parliament? Have you ever found an advertisement for a product so appealing that you wanted more information about it?

The style you use for letters like this is the personal business letter. It is personal because you are writing as an individual, not as an employee of a company. It is business because you are not writing to a friend.

In the TAKE ACTION activities you will have some opportunities to write a letter then mail it. You may be surprised at the results.

Yours sincerely,
Judi Misener

YOUR SIGNATURE

BEGINNING

MIDDLE

END

TAKE ACTION #3

A. One way to judge how well you communicate when you write a letter is by the type of reply you receive. The following activities ask you to write letters which you will then mail. Use the checklist below to help you write effective business letters for the following.

(i) Think about an item you have purchased that was unsatisfactory. Perhaps it broke easily or did not do all that the advertisement claimed. Write a letter complaining about the product and asking for a replacement or a refund. You must first decide where to write—the store where you purchased it or the company that made it (or both). Look up the telephone number in the telephone book and call to find out the correct mailing address and the name of the president of the company or the owner of the store.

(ii) Do you have a report or project to do in another class that needs information for which you have to write away? Use this time to write, asking for brochures, booklets, posters, etc., to help you succeed in your other class.

(iii) Bring in your favourite magazine. In most magazines, there will be free sample items to write away for or a product you would like to have more information on in case you want to purchase it. Write to one of the advertisers in your magazine. (Sometimes advertisements ask you to enclose a stamped, self-addressed envelope. If so, do not forget to do so.)

BUSINESS LETTERS CHECKLIST

To make a good impression, your letter should:

- ☐ look clean and neat.
- ☐ be evenly placed on the page.
- ☐ be signed neatly.
- ☐ sound sincere and courteous.
- ☐ make its purpose clear.
- ☐ be well organized.
- ☐ contain all necessary information.
- ☐ be concise.
- ☐ avoid jargon and clichés.
- ☐ be correct. (Check spelling, grammar, punctuation, typing, and mathematical calculations.)

(iv) Send a letter to the editor of your favourite magazine or your local newspaper. Say what you like and/or dislike about the publication or comment on a recent article or even suggest ideas for future articles. Someone will notify you if they are considering publishing your letter. If your letter is published, bring the magazine or newspaper to class.

(v) Write to someone who has a high profile job. You might, for example, write to your member of Parliament or your mayor, asking for their stands on a certain issue that concerns you. You could have some questions for an author of one of the books you are using this year. Have you always wanted to write to a famous entertainer? Now is your chance!

Addressing Envelopes

You will have to address an envelope for each of the letters you have written. The most common size of envelope for a business letter is a Number 10 envelope (105 mm x 242 mm). You can fold your letter in three and insert it easily into the envelope.

FOLDING LETTERS:

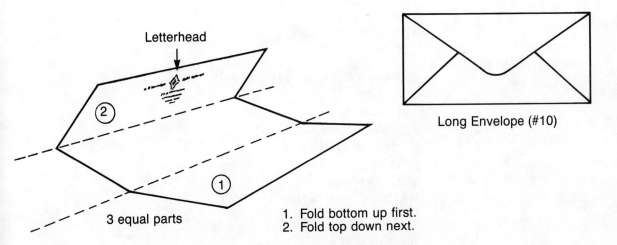

Letterhead

② ①

3 equal parts

Long Envelope (#10)

1. Fold bottom up first.
2. Fold top down next.

Handwritten envelopes are acceptable for personal business letters if you cannot type or do not have access to a typewriter.

Make sure the receiver's address is correct or the chances of your letter being delivered are poor. It is also very important that your address is correct so that the person to whom you write will know where to send a reply.

Business addresses should include if applicable:

- receiver's name
- receiver's position in the company
- name of firm
- name of building
- suite, office, or floor number
- street address
- post office box number
- postal station name
- city or town name in capital letters
- province, territory, or state (the complete name is preferred but standard abbreviations and two-letter codes are acceptable; see pp. 272-273.)
- postal code in capital letters and large numbers

EXAMPLES OF ADDRESSES

Business with post office box
Mr. J. Martin,
Personnel Manager,
General Computer Corporation,
P.O. Box 1000,
Postal Station A,
WINNIPEG, Manitoba
R3C 2M1

Business without post office box
R.P. Taylor,
Circulation Manager,
The Weekly Journal,
Confederation Building,
Suite 17,
10 Capital Square,
HALIFAX, Nova Scotia
B2K 1S3

Business with a street address
J. Dash,
President,
Powerboat Inc.,
23 Dennett Drive,
MONTREAL, Quebec
H4E 2C4

Personal Business Envelope

Your Name
Apartment Number Sender
Street Number and Name
Town, Province CODE

Special Mailing
Instructions

Receiver

Receiver's Name
Receiver's Company
Street Number and Name
Town, Province
POSTAL CODE

TAKE ACTION #4

A. Address an envelope for each of the letters you wrote in TAKE ACTION #3. Have your teacher evaluate each letter and envelope before you mail them. As the replies come back, discuss them as a class. Are they effective business letters? Why or why not?

Envelopes for formal business letters are always typed. A formal business envelope has a pre-printed logo and return address. Many companies also have a machine to stamp their letters.

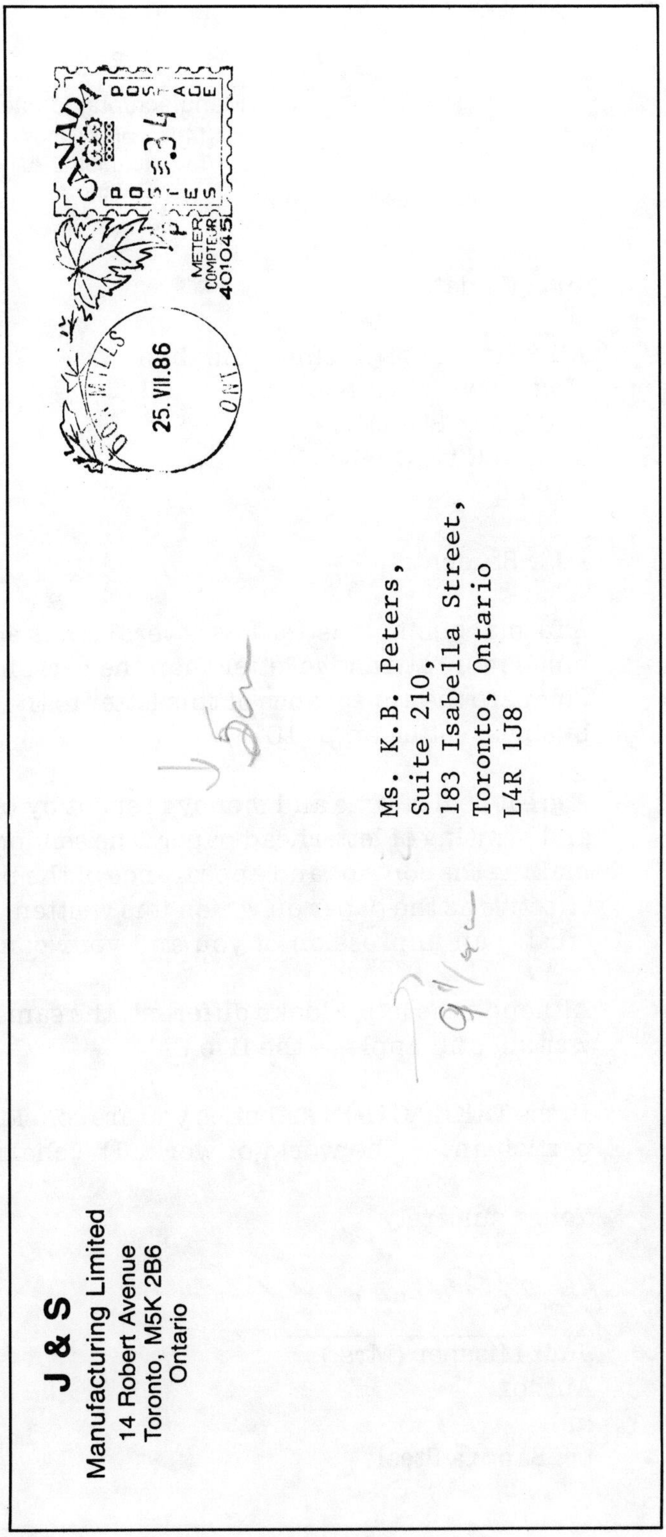

CANADA

P·O·S·T·E·S

P·O·S·T·A·G·E

$ 00 = 34

METER
COMPTEUR/S
4010451

25. VII.86

ONT

Ms. K.B. Peters,
Suite 210,
183 Isabella Street,
Toronto, Ontario
L4R 1J8

J & S

Manufacturing Limited
14 Robert Avenue
Toronto, M5K 2B6
Ontario

J & S
Manufacturing Limited
14 Robert Avenue
Toronto, M5K 2B6
Ontario

Today's date

All Students of Business English
Hometown High School
456 Mark Street
Quebec City, Quebec
G1P 2Q7

Dear Students

A formal business letter has several items added to it that make it a much more attractive letter than the personal business letter. Compare the appearance of this letter to that of the personal business letter on p. 107.

A great deal of time and money is spent by businesses in the design and printing of letterhead paper. The sender is responsible for making the content and appearance of the body of the letter as effective as the paper on which it is written. The letter you send creates an impression of you and your company.

Although the letter looks different, the same guidelines for good writing still apply — the five Cs!

In the TAKE ACTION activities you are considered to be a fully-fledged participant in the world of work. The challenge awaits you.

Yours sincerely

Judi Misener

Judi Misener (Mrs.)
Author
:mh
pc: Sandra Steele

The sequence of business letters often follows this pattern:
- letter of inquiry, request, or complaint (sender needs information or is complaining about a service or product)
- answer to the inquiry or complaint (receiver of first letter replies giving, if possible, the information requested)
- thank-you letter (good business etiquette encourages the use of thank-you letters)

PACIFIC TRAVEL

PACIFIC TRAVEL LTD.
29 ESSEX AVENUE
CHILLIWACK, BRITISH COLUMBIA
V9W 5E5

Mr. M. Dubois
Sales Manager
Sullivan Computer Systems Ltd.
1502 Lynden Dr.
New Westminster, British Columbia
V1P 6Z3

Dear Mr. Dubois

We recently purchased a 2500CL computer system from your company to use at our travel agency. While this new system has helped us improve our speed in making reservations for clients, we feel that a better working knowledge of the system would help us to obtain maximum use and efficiency.

Would it be possible for you to supply us with some more information about other available applications for the 2500CL system? Perhaps you have a brochure or pamphlet you could send us.

We would appreciate any information you can give us.

Yours sincerely

M. McKelvie

M. McKelvie (Ms.)
Office Manager

SULLIVAN COMPUTER SYSTEMS LTD.
1502 LYNDEN DRIVE,
NEW WESTMINSTER, BRITISH COLUMBIA
V1P 6Z3

Ms. M. McKelvie
Office Manager
Pacific Travel Ltd.
29 Essex Avenue
Chilliwack, British Columbia
V9W 5E5

Dear Ms. McKelvie

Thank you for your recent letter expressing interest in making maximum use of your new 2500CL system.

I have enclosed several booklets which outline the working procedures and other applications of this system. I hope they are of some assistance to you.

Our sales representative in your area, Kim Lheong, has suggested that you might also be interested in a seminar that the system manufacturer provides to customers. The seminar deals with all aspects of the 2500CL and was designed for people with little or no computer experience.

If you feel a workshop like this would benefit you and/or your employees, we would be happy to arrange it for you. Kim will be calling on you within the next week. Please let her know if you would like to participate in this seminar or if you have any other questions or concerns.

We appreciate your interest in our products. If we can be of any further assistance, please let us know.

Yours sincerely

M. Dubois

M. Dubois
Sales Manager

PACIFIC TRAVEL

PACIFIC TRAVEL LTD.
29 ESSEX AVENUE
CHILLIWACK, BRITISH COLUMBIA
V9W 5E5

Mr. M. Dubois
Sales Manager
Sullivan Computer Systems
1502 Lynden Dr.
New Westminster, British Columbia
V1P 6Z3

Dear Mr. Dubois

Thank you for your prompt reply to my request for more information on the 2500CL computer system.

The pamphlets you sent were very useful and your sales representative, Kim Lheong, was most helpful in answering my questions.

As you suggested, we arranged to have the manufacturer's seminar given to our employees. It was very interesting and informative, and many of our staff have noted they feel much more comfortable working with the system. I think this will really help to improve efficiency and productivity.

Thank you again for all your help.

Yours sincerely

M. McKelvie (Ms.)
Office Manager

TAKE ACTION #5

A. Read the three sample request, answer to the request, and thank-you letters (pp. 116, 117, 118). Write your own sequence of three letters. Your first letter should be a letter of complaint to a business. Your next letter requires that you become the receiver of the first letter and answer yourself. Write the third letter thanking the company for satisfactorily handling your complaint.

We hope your first two letters are not like these.

Letter of Complaint
Gents: I ordered one of them engines on page 777 and it doesn't work. Please send me one of them gasoline engines you show on page 785 and if it's any good I'll send you a cheque for it.

Company Reply
Dear Sir: Please return your first engine. Also, please send us your cheque and if it's any good, we'll send you the other engine.

TAKE ACTION ON THE JOB #2

A. Ask your supervisor if you may bring in samples of your company's letterhead paper and printed envelopes. Set up a display in your classroom.

Most companies receive large quantities of mail daily. Your letter must stand out from the others. One way to do this is to keep your letter as brief as possible. A busy person will appreciate not having to read extra material which wastes time. Some people won't bother to start reading a letter if it looks too long.

This story says it all:

If you have to write a letter, keep it brief and to the point. Glen Kerfoot is a business communications consultant who believes that business letters should be as brief as possible. He once illustrated the point during an after-dinner talk with several effective letters containing just one sentence each. Shortly afterward he received a letter from the group which contained one word: '**Thanks.**'

For the next several years he displayed the one-word letter at his talks to show that one word could be a complete communication, also stating that one word had to be the absolute minimum.

One day, after addressing the Lexington Chapter of the Administrative Management Association he received the following letter:

Dear Mr. Kerfoot:

Appreciatively yours,

J. Edward Musser
President

From *Fat Paper: Diets for Trimming Paperwork*, Lee Grossman

SALES AND COLLECTION LETTERS

Two types of letters that are formal business letters and rarely written as a personal letter are the sales letter and the collection letter.

It is most important that a sales letter accomplish these four things:

- attract the receiver's attention
- create a desire for the product or service
- convince the receiver that the product or service is the best of its kind
- motivate action — make a sale!

ONTARIO SMALL BUSINESS ASSOCIATION

August 17, 19__

Ms. B. Filicetti
41 Norfolk St.
Toronto, Ont.
M5X 2L7

Dear Ms. Filicetti

How would you like to lose your job . . . and start a new business?

Many people talk about setting up their own companies but sometimes they just don't know where to start. If you would like the freedom and independence of being your own boss, working your own hours, and setting your own standards, we can help you.

The Ontario Small Business Association is sponsoring a weekend workshop which will bring together some of the most experienced and successful self-starters in the business community to give you advice on starting your own company. These experts will cover such topics as capital investment, market research, accounting procedures, legal advice, employment practices, and all the things you'll need to know to be a self-employed success.

This series of workshops and seminars will be held at the Central Convention Centre the weekend of October 24-25. If you're interested in learning more, please fill out the enclosed form and mail it to us.

After all, what have you got to lose?

Yours truly,

Pam Friday

Pam Friday
Promotions Officer

TAKE ACTION #6

A. Read the sample sales letter on p. 121. Write your own letter selling a membership to a health club, a lawn maintenance service, a series of books on a specific subject (e.g., sewing, woodworking), or a product of your own choice that is approved by your teacher.

A collection letter is sent to a company or individual who has not paid a bill on time. Remember that you want the individual to pay the bill. Do not offend the receiver or you might never see your money! Many businesses send out a series of collection letters—each one getting a little stronger in its demand for payment.

TAKE ACTION #7

A. Read the sample collection letters below and on p. 123. Write a collection letter requesting payment of an overdue account.

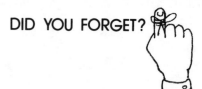

DID YOU FORGET?

Say Mr. Smith,
    Are you still running around with my cheque in your pocket? Just a reminder — your balance of $48.26 is still owing.

Dear Ms. Brown:

We were pleased to receive your recent order for two lawn chairs. We have them in stock.

We shall be happy to send them to you upon receipt of your cheque for $50.60 which is the overdue balance on your account.

Possibly you have overlooked this matter when mailing out your monthly cheques.

Gentlemen:

Our records show that your account has an outstanding balance of $598.76. As we have had no reply to our previous requests for payment, we must now resort to legal action.

If you have not come to some arrangement with our accounting department within 15 days, we will be handing over your account to our lawyers.

TAKE ACTION ON THE JOB #3

A. Ask your supervisor for the opportunity to write a letter on her/his behalf. Show your letter to your supervisor before you mail it. Your supervisor will evaluate it and approve it for mailing.

B. Ask your supervisor for permission to bring to class samples of business letters received by your company as well as the replies written to those letters. You might be required to remove some of the information in the letters (such as the receiver's address). The content of the letter is all that is required. Read the letters to the class and assess the effectiveness of each one.

FORM LETTERS

Another type of business letter is the form letter. This is used when many people are to receive the same message with perhaps only one or two different pieces of information contained in each letter. A form letter is much cheaper than writing an original letter to each individual. Only a few years ago, most of these letters were typed once with blank spaces left in them for the different information required. They were duplicated by being photocopied or run off on a stencil machine. The person's name, address, and other information were then typed in as required.

Today, most form letters are done on a word processor which can be programmed to insert the required information in the letter as it is being printed. Each person receives an original typed letter. This makes the letter appear to be more personal than the old style of form letter.

The word processor is also used to generate addresses on envelopes for each individual receiving a letter. To simplify the process further and save the company money, window envelopes and computerized address labels are often used. To use a window envelope, you fold the letter so the inside address shows through the window. This means that an envelope does not have to be typed.

TAKE ACTION #8
A. Your school librarian needs a form letter to be sent to students who have not returned their library books. Write a letter which could be used for this purpose. Indicate where information would vary on each letter.

B. (i) You have your own business. Design a letterhead that you would use. Decide on a name, an address, a logo design, and how it should look on the letter paper. Letterheads can also include telephone and telex numbers as well as slogans. Check the display you made in Take Action on the Job #2 (p. 119) for ideas for your letterhead.

(ii) Using your own letterhead, write a collection letter that could be used as a form letter for customers whose balances are overdue. Leave blanks to indicate how much they owe and how many months overdue their payments are.

TAKE ACTION ON THE JOB #4
A. With permission from your supervisor, bring in sample form letters that are used by your company.

B. Ask if your company needs a new form letter or would like a current form letter revised. Offer to write one and bring your sample to class.

THE SIXTH C OF BUSINESS WRITING
Posters, notices, brochures, and company newsletters are forms of written communication that are also used in business. The five Cs still apply but a sixth C can be included—**creativity**. Let your imagination take over.

WE WANT YOU!!

WHY?   To attend the Personnel Department's Family BBQ
WHEN?   July 1   2:00 p.m.
WHERE? Bruce's Mills Conservation Area
            (map to follow)

PRIZES!   PRIZES!

SWIMMING, BASEBALL, RACES
Don't delay, reply today to
JoAnne Grayson,
ext. 29

THE BUCKLEY BULLETIN — Summer Edition

Luckily July 1—Canada's Birthday and the Personnel department's family BBQ—was a beautiful, sunny day.

The Ferdinand family proved to be the fastest on their feet and cleaned up at the races.

Bill's Baseball Bats battled hard to win the game but the champions for the second year in a row are the Personnel Pirates, coached by Error-free Erin! Congratulations!

Our beloved president, Mr. Rosetti, was truly "all wet" after being dunked in the pond.

Full of food, fun, and lots of sun, we all look forward to next year's picnic.

Suzanne Hotson

TAKE ACTION #9
A. Examine the list of office rules from the 1800s on p. 126. Design a poster with rules that apply to the office of today.

Office Staff Practices (1852)

1. Godliness, Cleanliness, and Punctuality are the necessities of a good business.

2. This firm has reduced the hours of work, and the Clerical Staff will now only have to be present between the hours of 7 a.m. and 6 p.m. weekdays.

3. Daily prayers will be held each morning in the Main Office. The Clerical Staff will be present.

4. Clothing must be of a sober nature. The Clerical Staff will not disport themselves in raiment of bright colours nor will they wear hose, unless in good repair.

5. Overshoes and top coats may be worn in the office, but neck scarves and headwear may be worn in inclement weather.

6. A stove is provided for the benefit of the Clerical Staff. Coal and wood must be kept in the locker. It is recommended that each member of the Clerical Staff bring 4 pounds of coal, each day, during cold weather.

7. No member of the Clerical Staff may leave the room without permission from Mr. Rogers. The calls of nature are permitted, and Clerical Staff may use the garden below the second gate. This area must be kept in good order.

8. No talking allowed during business hours.

9. The craving of tobacco, wine or spirits is a human weakness and, as such, is forbidden to all members of the Clerical Staff.

10. Now that the hours of business have been drastically reduced, the partaking of food is allowed between 11:30 a.m. and noon, but work will not on any account cease.

11. Members of the Clerical Staff will provide their own pens. A new sharpener is available, on application to Mr. Rogers.

12. Mr. Rogers will nominate a Senior Clerk to be responsible for the cleanliness of the Main Office and the private office, and all Boys and Juniors will report to him 40 minutes before prayers, and will remain after closing hours for similar work. Brushes, brooms, scrubbers and soap are provided by the owners.

13. The new increased weekly wages are as hereunder detailed-

Junior Boys (10-11 years)....1-4d.   Junior Clerks ....8-7d.
Boys (to 14 years).........2-1d.   Clerks...........10-9d.
Juniors..............4-3d.   Senior Clerks (after 15 years with the owners)....21-

The owners recognize the generosity of the New Labour Laws, but will expect a great rise in output of work to compensate near Utopian conditions.

B. You are going to publish a class newsletter to cover a month's events and activities at your school.

(i) There are several steps you will need to follow:

- Decide on the organization of your newsletter (e.g., what to call it, what activities should be covered).
- Decide on a publication date and deadlines for articles.
- Appoint an editorial board to whom all finished articles will be submitted.
- Appoint a publication team to arrange for the physical preparation of the newsletter (e.g., arranging to use the word processing equipment in the business department).
- Assign pairs or teams of reporters to cover specific activities (e.g., dances, club meetings, sporting events, student council meetings). Remember that as well as reporting on this month's events, your newsletter should include notices about forthcoming activities.

(ii) Work with your partner or team to prepare your article. Submit your final version to the editorial board by the due date.

(iii) When your newsletter has been prepared and printed, distribute copies to students or post copies on school bulletin boards.

TAKE ACTION ON THE JOB #5
A. Contribute an article to your company newsletter outlining how you feel as a co-operative education student or part-time employee of the company. If your company does not have a newsletter, you might want to organize one!

FORMS

The worlds of business, government, and industry at times seem to run on the power of the form. In the chapter on listening you completed several business forms used when taking down information over the phone. There are hundreds of other forms that you will have to complete—forms to get a driver's licence, a licence plate, insurance for your car, life and health insurance, bank accounts, credit cards, jobs, a social insurance number, a mortgage, and one to get married. You can probably think of many more.

Different forms often require the same information. Hunting up the same documents and information each time you complete a form is time-consuming and frustrating. A personal data sheet will prevent this.

MasterCard Application

PLEASE PRINT CLEARLY AND COMPLETE IN FULL

Bank of Montreal

06

| ☐ Mr. ☐ Mrs. ☐ Miss ☐ Dr. ☐ Ms. | First Name | Middle Initials | Last Name | Home ( ) | Telephone Office ( ) |

| Present Address | Apartment Number | City | Province | Postal Code |

| Years at present address | Own ☐ | Rent ☐ | Other ☐ | Monthly rent or mortgage $ | Date of birth M /D /Y |

| Previous address | | How long? | ☐ Married ☐ Single | ☐ Divorced | ☐ Separated ☐ Widowed |

| Present occupation | | Gross **monthly** salary $ | Other **monthly** income $ |

| Spouse's name | | Number of dependents (excluding spouse) |

| Name and address of present employer | | How long? |

| Previous occupation | Previous employer and address | How long? |

| Spouse's occupation | Name and address of spouse's employer | How long? | Gross **monthly** salary $ |

| Name of nearest relative not living with you | Address | Relationship | Chequing Account Number |

| Where do you bank? | Address of branch (and transit number if known) | Savings Account Number |

Name	Creditor	Address	**Credit references** Loan/Account number	Original amount	Balance owing	Monthly payments

| Home mortgaged by | Estimated value $ | Mortgage amount $ | Amount owing $ |

| Car year and make | | Province | Drivers Licence | Number |

Apply for a card for your spouse too!
Simply have your husband or wife sign this application in the space below.

| | Correspondence ☐ English ☐ French | Send statement to ☐ Home ☐ Office |

You will automatically receive a Personal Identification Number (PIN) to access your MasterCard account through Instabank.

If you wish to access your Bank of Montreal accounts, please see your branch after you receive your MasterCard card and PIN.

The undersigned or each of them, if more than one, certifies the above information to be true and correct, requests a Bank of Montreal MasterCard card and renewals or replacements thereof from time to time at the Bank's discretion, requests a Personal Identification Number (PIN) in order to allow use of the card in Bank of Montreal Instabank units and, if available, other automated banking machine systems. **BY SIGNING BELOW ACCEPTS AS NOTICE IN WRITING OF AND CONSENTS TO THE OBTAINING FROM ANY CREDIT REPORTING AGENCY OR ANY CREDIT GRANTOR SUCH INFORMATION AS THE BANK MAY REQUIRE AT ANY TIME IN CONNECTION WITH THE CREDIT HEREBY APPLIED FOR,** consents to the disclosure at any time of any information concerning the undersigned to any credit reporting agency or to any credit grantor with whom the undersigned has financial relations and, if a MasterCard is issued, agrees to abide by the terms and conditions of the Bank of Montreal MasterCard Cardholder Agreement accompanying the MasterCard card.
If an additional card is requested in spouse's name, each of the undersigned agrees to be jointly and severally liable for indebtedness incurred through use of MasterCard cards issued pursuant to this application and authorizes through use of such cards deposits to and withdrawals from bank accounts designated by either of the undersigned.

X _____

Signature of spouse (if card wanted)   Date

X _____

Signature of applicant

An application for a MasterCard credit card. Accuracy is important when you fill out forms—always check if you are unsure about something.

▮✦ Employment and Emploi et
Immigration Canada Immigration Canada

CERTIFICATION STAMP

APPLICATION FOR A SOCIAL INSURANCE NUMBER OR REPLACEMENT OF SOCIAL INSURANCE NUMBER CARD
NOT TO BE USED TO AMEND SOCIAL INSURANCE RECORDS
(USE FORM EMP 2121)

→ DO NOT WRITE IN THESE SPACES →

PRINT IN DARK INK OR USE TYPEWRITER
LEAD PENCIL NOT ACCEPTED

18

| 1 NAME TO BE SHOWN ON CARD | FIRST NAME | MIDDLE NAME | PRESENT FAMILY NAME (SURNAME) |

2 DATE OF BIRTH — DAY MONTH YEAR DO NOT WRITE HERE
3 SEX MALE ☐ FEMALE ☐ TWIN ☐
4 MOTHER'S MAIDEN NAME

5 FATHER'S FULL NAME
6 PLACE OF BIRTH (CITY, TOWN, VILLAGE, PROVINCE, COUNTRY)

7 FAMILY NAME AT BIRTH
8 OTHER FAMILY NAME(S) FORMERLY USED   DO NOT WRITE HERE

9 HAVE YOU EVER BEFORE APPLIED FOR OR RECEIVED A SOCIAL INSURANCE NUMBER YES ☐ NO ☐
10 IF "YES" WRITE YOUR NUMBER HERE AND INCLUDE CURRENT FEE   DON'T KNOW

11 MARITAL STATUS SINGLE ☐ MARRIED ☐ OTHER ☐
12 STATUS IN CANADA CANADIAN CITIZEN ☐ STATUS INDIAN ☐ PERMANENT RESIDENT ☐ OTHER ☐
13 AREA CODE TELEPHONE NO

14 YOUR MAILING ADDRESS (NO AND STREET)   (CITY, TOWN, VILLAGE)   (PROVINCE)   (POSTAL CODE)

15 APPLICANT'S SIGNATURE AND DATE
16 IF MARK X IS USED AS SIGNATURE IN BOX 15 HAVE 2 WITNESSES SIGN HERE
FIRST WITNESS   SECOND WITNESS

17 ALL NAMES AS SHOWN ON PRIMARY DOCUMENT (FOR LOCAL OFFICE USE ONLY)   SURNAME   PRIMARY DOCUMENTS SEC./SUPP.

DO NOT WRITE IN THESE SPACES (FOR CENTRAL INDEX USE ONLY)   FEE PAID IF REPLACEMENT CARD ☐

INFORMATION COLLECTED ON THIS FORM IS USED FOR THE PURPOSE OF ISSUING SOCIAL INSURANCE NUMBERS. ITS COLLECTION IS AUTHORIZED BY THE UNEMPLOYMENT INSURANCE ACT. FOR MORE DETAILS ON THE USES AND RIGHTS CONCERNING INSPECTION AND CORRECTION OF THE INFORMATION, REFER TO THE PERSONAL INFORMATION INDEX AND IN PARTICULAR TO BANK NO. EIC P560, AVAILABLE AT POST OFFICES.

NOTE: IT IS A CRIMINAL OFFENCE TO KNOWINGLY APPLY FOR MORE THAN ONE SOCIAL INSURANCE NO. YOU ARE NOT PERMITTED TO GIVE OR LEND YOUR CARD TO ANYONE.

IMPORTANT ▶ **YOUR SOCIAL INSURANCE CARD WILL BE MAILED TO YOU AT THE ADDRESS THAT YOU PRINT BELOW**

TAKE CARE OF YOUR CARD. IT IS VALUABLE.
COPY YOUR NUMBER HERE
AND KEEP FOR YOUR RECORDS

NAME	
ADDRESS	
CITY, PROVINCE	
POSTAL CODE	

YOUR SOCIAL INSURANCE NUMBER IS

THIS NUMBER IS ISSUED IN YOUR NAME ONLY

Canada**▮✦**

EMP 2120 (12-84)

(FRANÇAIS AU VERSO)

Some applications forms, such as this one for a Social Insurance Number, are accompanied by a list of instructions or tips on filling them out.

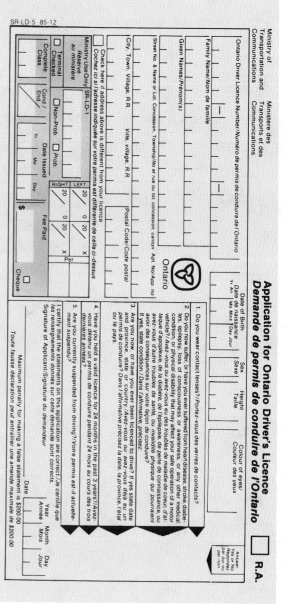

An application for an Ontario
driver's licence. In some provinces
application forms are no longer
used.

TAKE ACTION #10

A. Prepare a personal data sheet using the following as a guide. Print the headings and information neatly. As with any form of written communication, the appearance of a form makes an impression on the receiver.

Print the required information after each heading. If you do not know the information, leave space and put it in later.

When you use your data sheet to fill out other forms, remember that not all forms are the same. Some information may not be arranged the way it is on your personal data sheet. Always read forms carefully before you complete them.

Name—Usually your last name goes first, then your first name, followed by an initial; e.g., "Misener, Judith E." if the form is a legal document and "Misener, Judi E." if it is not.

Date of Birth (sometimes shown as D.O.B.)—It is usually written day, month, year. Use the numeric method; e.g., 13 03 19__. When you fill out other forms, read the form carefully to see in which order it should be written.

Address—Be sure to include apartment number if applicable and always include your postal code. Again, when you fill out other forms, check to see which line your street address appears on and where you should write the town, the province, and the postal code.

Municipality, Region, Township—Find out which one you live in and how to spell it correctly.

Telephone Number—Know your area code as well as the number; e.g., (416) 555-1111

Social Insurance Number (sometimes shown as S.I.N.)—Make sure you have nine numbers; e.g., 123 456 789

Parents' Names, Addresses, and Phone Numbers—Use the names of your step-parents, foster parents, or guardian if applicable. Some forms may also ask for your mother's maiden name. Include both personal and business addresses and phone numbers. This information can be used if you are asked for next of kin or whom to contact in case of an emergency. Next of kin means your closest living relative.

Schools Attended—List all the schools you have attended including their addresses. Beside each one, put down the years you attended it. Start with the first school you attended and continue to the one you are attending now.

Graduation Year — Indicate month as well as year.

Employment History—List all the places you have worked, starting from your first job. Include your employer's name, employer's position, address, and telephone number. Include such activities as babysitting and delivering papers as well as any other part-time jobs you may have held.

Bank Accounts—Know your account numbers and the address of your bank. Include the branch identification number.

Signature—Decide how you wish to sign your name. Always sign the same way each time you are asked for your signature.

B. Bring as many forms as you can find to class. Complete the forms using the information from your personal data sheet and add them to your writing folder. Some forms you may find easily are passport applications (available at passport offices, post offices, and some travel agencies), social insurance number applications (available at Canada Employment Centres), and credit card applications (available at banks).

TAKE ACTION ON THE JOB #6
A. Try to find out where the forms that your company uses are designed. If possible, talk to the designers, asking them how forms are developed. Talk to the people who use the information on the completed forms and ask them how forms assist them with their jobs. Write a report on your findings.

B. With permission from your supervisor, bring in as many sample forms as you can from your company. The forms can be duplicated for the class for further practice or set up in a bulletin board display. (See copyright notice on p. ix .)

THE BUSINESS OF SPEAKING

6

Talking and eloquence are not the same thing: to speak, and to speak well, are two things.
BEN JONSON

TAKE NOTE

In verbal communication feedback is often immediate. Feedback from your audience may be verbal or non-verbal. By listening to and watching your audience, you can clear up any questions, re-emphasize certain points you are making, expand your presentation to include more information if necessary, or eliminate parts of your presentation. Verbal communication allows you flexibility to respond to feedback.

Does the title of this chapter make you feel nervous or anxious? Do you have visions of standing up and speaking to your class, trying desperately to remember a long speech on an unfamiliar topic? Well, take a deep breath and relax. This chapter concentrates on voice control, use of the business telephone, conversations, and small, prepared talks using props and notes.

VOICE CONTROL

In chapter 1 you were briefly introduced to the importance of voice control as a communication tool. To refresh your memory, voice control includes:

- intonation
- pitch
- volume of speech
- pace
- clarity
- voice quality

A clear, positive voice is essential in business—for face to face communication, presentations, and especially for telephone communication. You must sound confident, interested, and enthusiastic.

It is important to discover how you sound now and work at improving any weaknesses you may identify.

TAKE ACTION #1

A. You are going to complete a personal voice profile. Record your voice as you read a passage from a book or magazine. Play back the tape in a quiet place. Your teacher will give you a copy of the voice analysis checklist on p. 138 to help you create your personal voice profile.

B. Bring your tape to class. Working in groups of three, listen to each person's tape and complete a voice analysis for each member of your group. Compare your original profile with those done by your group. There may be some disagreements—discuss these in your group and prepare a final personal voice profile chart for yourself which includes all the comments you agree are appropriate.

Now that you know the areas where you can improve or further strengthen your voice, it is important that you continue to work on how you sound. Tape your voice, say once every two weeks, using the voice analysis checklist after each session. Compare your checklists to judge your improvement.

Many careers depend almost entirely on good voice control. The more obvious ones are those of disc jockey or television announcer. What others can you think of?

TAKE ACTION #2

A. Listen to a radio in class, comparing announcers from different stations. Evaluate each one using your checklist then hold a class discussion to reach a consensus as to the most desirable voice qualities. Prepare a list of these and post it in your classroom for easy reference over the coming weeks.

We spend 30 per cent of our communication speaking, so good voice control is important. In some professions, it is essential.

VOICE ANALYSIS CHECKLIST

Rate each component on a scale from 1 (Needs Improvement) to 10 (Excellent)—a rating of 6 would mean Satisfactory. Add up your ratings to find your total score.

INTONATION — Is the inflection and emphasis monotonous, sing-song, or expressive?

1	2	3	4	5	6	7	8	9	10

PITCH — Is it too high, too low, or appropriate?

1	2	3	4	5	6	7	8	9	10

VOLUME — Is it too loud, too soft, inconsistent, or appropriate?

1	2	3	4	5	6	7	8	9	10

PACE — Is it too fast, too slow, or appropriate?

1	2	3	4	5	6	7	8	9	10

CLARITY

Enunciation — Are the individual words clear?

1	2	3	4	5	6	7	8	9	10

Pronunciation — Is it correct?

1	2	3	4	5	6	7	8	9	10

QUALITY OF VOICE — Is the tone harsh, thin, or resonant?

1	2	3	4	5	6	7	8	9	10

TOTAL SCORE: _____

1 –39 Needs Improvement
40–55 Satisfactory
56–64 Good
65–70 Excellent

COMMENTS: _____
_____
_____
_____

THE BUSINESS TELEPHONE

TAKE NOTE
Voice control is most important when you use the telephone —
your other non-verbal skills cannot be seen. When you
communicate by telephone, your voice is the only medium for
expressing your personality and creating a favourable
impression on the person receiving your call.

All business people use the phone and every one should know how
to use it well. When you speak, visualize the person to whom you
are talking. Smile as you speak—it shows in your voice and
enables you to sound sincere and interested in the person on the
other end of the line.

Smiling while you speak shows in
your voice and helps you develop
a pleasant telephone manner.

Before you make a telephone call, organize your desk so that you have everything you need.

It is important to plan your phone calls before you make them.

- Always have paper and pens or pencils ready.
- Read any correspondence or notes from previous calls to or from the person or company.
- Have any information you might need (e.g., a company's file or a customer's order) ready on your desk.
- List questions you wish to ask and prepare headings for information you require.
- Make sure you know the name (and the proper pronunciation) of the person you need to speak to and what you want to say.

As you learned in "The Business of Listening," it is important to make notes during the conversation. If you have made a list of questions or headings, you can fill in the information there. When you are finished the call, record what action, if any, needs to be taken and place your notes in the file for future reference.

TAKE ACTION #3
A. With a partner, write a business telephone script for one of the following situations. First plan the questions and the information the situation requires, then write the dialogue.

(i) A very important order for specialized tools was not delivered on time. This delay caused the loss of an important customer and several thousand dollars worth of business. One of you will represent the customer who placed the order and the other will represent the company which did not deliver the tools on time.

(ii) The photocopier in your office is constantly jamming with paper. Decide which partner will place the call requesting a service visit and which partner will represent the company which services the photocopier.

(iii) A company needs to place an order for several items used in business. Decide what the items will be. You will be ordering the items from a catalogue.

B. Perform your call for the class.

C. Analyse each telephone conversation using the copies of the checklist on p. 144 that your teacher will give you. As a class, discuss any problems you encountered and suggest possible solutions.

D. Using the Yellow Pages, make a list of five companies that are in the same line of work. Phone each of them and ask for the correct mailing address and the name of the head of the company. As you are doing this, record the information you are given. Describe your first impression of the company. Indicate which of the five companies you would do business with, based on your impressions from the phone calls.

E. Examine Bell Canada's "Test your telephone habits" on p. 145. As a class, use Bell's test as a model to make up your own list of telephone rules. Place your completed list in your writing folder.

F. Using your list, evaluate the telephone habits you practise at home.

TAKE ACTION ON THE JOB #1

A. Write a report on how the telephone is used at your place of business; for example, who answers incoming calls, what people say when they answer the phone, how inter-office phones are answered, whether there are regulations on personal use of the phone during business hours or on placing long distance calls. Describe the type of equipment that is used in your place of business and how much it differs from your home system.

B. If your company has a manual on telephone use, ask your supervisor for permission to bring a copy to class. Report on the contents of the manual to your class.

C. Use your list of rules to analyse your telephone habits while at work. How do your habits at work compare to your telephone habits at home?

Advanced technology has increased our use of the telephone in business.

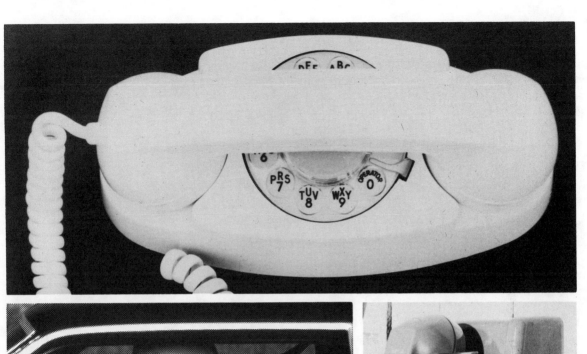

TELEPHONE CONVERSATION CHECKLIST

Rate each component on a scale from 1 (Needs Improvement) to 10 (Excellent)—a rating of 6 would mean Satisfactory. Add up your ratings to find your total score.

INTONATION — Is the inflection and emphasis monotonous, sing-song, or expressive?

| 1 | 2 | 3 | 4 | 5 | 6 | 7 | 8 | 9 | 10 |

PITCH — Is it too high, too low, or appropriate?

| 1 | 2 | 3 | 4 | 5 | 6 | 7 | 8 | 9 | 10 |

VOLUME — Is it too loud, too soft, inconsistent, or appropriate?

| 1 | 2 | 3 | 4 | 5 | 6 | 7 | 8 | 9 | 10 |

PACE — Is it too fast, too slow, or appropriate?

| 1 | 2 | 3 | 4 | 5 | 6 | 7 | 8 | 9 | 10 |

CLARITY

Enunciation — Are the individual words clear?

| 1 | 2 | 3 | 4 | 5 | 6 | 7 | 8 | 9 | 10 |

Pronunciation — Is it correct?

| 1 | 2 | 3 | 4 | 5 | 6 | 7 | 8 | 9 | 10 |

QUALITY OF VOICE — Is the tone harsh, thin, or resonant?

| 1 | 2 | 3 | 4 | 5 | 6 | 7 | 8 | 9 | 10 |

LEVEL OF LANGUAGE — Is it too technical, too formal or informal, or appropriate?

| 1 | 2 | 3 | 4 | 5 | 6 | 7 | 8 | 9 | 10 |

OVERALL EFFECT — Were the speakers confident, helpful, pleasant, enthusiastic or uncertain, impersonal, or abrupt?

| 1 | 2 | 3 | 4 | 5 | 6 | 7 | 8 | 9 | 10 |

TOTAL SCORE: _____

1 –49 Needs Improvement
50–64 Satisfactory
65–79 Good
80–90 Excellent

COMMENTS: _____
_____
_____
_____

TEST YOUR TELEPHONE HABITS
Check The Answer That Best Applies

	Always Do	Usually Do	Seldom Do
1. Before leaving my phone, I leave word where I am going and when I plan to return.	☐	☐	☐
2. I answer my own phone whenever possible. I answer promptly . . . before the second ring.	☐	☐	☐
3. I identify myself at the beginning of the conversation whether I am taking or placing the call.	☐	☐	☐
4. I take care to speak directly into the telephone . . . clearly, naturally and pleasantly.	☐	☐	☐
5. I try to personalize my conversation by using the caller's name at every opportunity.	☐	☐	☐
6. I try to be informative when taking calls for others.	☐	☐	☐
7. I offer my help and assistance to the caller.	☐	☐	☐
8. When taking messages, I note all essential information and, if necessary, double check it.	☐	☐	☐
9. If it is necessary for the caller to wait longer than a minute while I leave the line, I offer to return the call.	☐	☐	☐
10. I thank the party for calling.	☐	☐	☐
11. I return all calls promptly.	☐	☐	☐
12. I treat all kinds of messages as important calls.	☐	☐	☐
13. I place my own local and long distance calls and I stay on the line while they are going through.	☐	☐	☐
14. I dial long distance calls direct whenever possible.	☐	☐	☐
15. When I need to place calls through the operator, I call by number.	☐	☐	☐

SCORING

Give yourself 4 points for every "always do" answer; 2 points for every "usually do," no points for "seldom do."

60-52 (TOP SCORE)

Nice going! Your telephone personality is winning friends for you.

51-42

Not bad! But added effort will bring big rewards.

BELOW 42

You're slipping! Concentrate on forming better telephone habits. Keep this test — take again in two weeks.

CONVERSATION

Reprinted by permission of United Feature Syndicate, Inc.

Your role in conversations continually changes from sender to receiver and back again. No longer are you relying only on voice control. You must make use of all your communication skills.

As both a sender and receiver in face to face conversation, concentrate on:

- being interested and attentive. You can show this through the use of eye contact, facial expressions, and posture. Remember that you are talking with, not at, someone.
- giving the other person room. Do not crowd each other. Keep approximately one to two metres between you.
- using good voice control.
- being honest and sincere—naturally. Acting naturally builds an atmosphere of trust and acceptance.
- being considerate. Do not interrupt, monopolize the conversation, or over-use the word "I."

Crowding people can make them uncomfortable and hinder effective communication. Watch for non-verbal clues that may indicate you are not giving the other person enough room.

TAKE NOTE
Business conversations, like all business communications, can vary from informal to formal, depending on the participants (audience) and the reasons for the conversation (purpose).

As with written communications, spoken communications have a definite structure—a beginning, a middle, and a conclusion. A conversation often begins when two people are introduced. For this reason introductions are important.

INTRODUCTIONS
There are certain rules you should follow when introducing people. People in positions of lower authority are always introduced to people in positions of higher authority. If shaking hands is in order, it is the person in the position of higher authority who should initiate it. However, if anyone in an introduction offers to shake hands, you should do so. You should also, when appropriate, identify people by their titles or positions, as well as by name.

Some examples of introductions are:

"Mr. Heath, I'd like to introduce Mrs. Kisluk, our new sales representative from J&S Manufacturing."
"How do you do, Mr. Heath?"
"How do you do, Mrs. Kisluk?"

"Ms. Lee, I'd like you to meet Mr. Valerio, our new employee in Research and Development. Ms. Lee is the supervisor of the Accounting Department."
"It's very nice to meet you, Ms. Lee."
"Thank you, Mr. Valerio. It's nice to meet you."

TAKE ACTION #4

A. Working in groups of three, practise making introductions in the following situations. Each group member will role-play a part.

(i) A new friend of the opposite sex is introduced to a parent.

(ii) A parent is introduced by a child to the child's teacher.

(iii) A personnel manager introduces a new employee to the shop steward.

B. As a class make a list of phrases and hints for introductions to post in your classroom.

SUSTAINING CONVERSATIONS

Often after introductions have been made you must carry on a conversation. Sustaining conversations involves hard work and the use of all your communication skills. It is important to keep a conversation interesting, informative, and productive.

TAKE ACTION #5

A. Your teacher will select a partner for you. With that partner, carry on a conversation about what your day has been like so far. Concentrate on all your communication skills (verbal and non-verbal) both as a listener and as a speaker. After five minutes of conversing, complete a copy of the conversation checklist (p. 156), then discuss with your partner how you felt about each other's communication skills. Suggest ways in which you and your partner might improve communication skills.

B. Choose a different partner and repeat the same activity.

C. Using your checklists, compare the two conversations. Was one easier than the other? How did they compare in level of language, content, proportion of time spent speaking and listening, and level of interest and productivity? As a class, discuss possible reasons for any differences.

CONVERSATION CHECKLIST

Rate each component on a scale from 1 (Needs Improvement) to 10 (Excellent)—a rating of 6 would mean Satisfactory. Add up your ratings to find your total score.

VOICE CONTROL — Rate the intonation, pitch, volume, pace, clarity, and voice quality.

1	2	3	4	5	6	7	8	9	10

BODY LANGUAGE — Is the speaker's body language effective?

1	2	3	4	5	6	7	8	9	10

INTRODUCTION — Is it smooth and friendly, or awkward?

1	2	3	4	5	6	7	8	9	10

LEVEL OF LANGUAGE — Is it too technical, too formal or informal, or appropriate?

1	2	3	4	5	6	7	8	9	10

LISTENING SKILLS — Does the person listen attentively and respond accurately to other's comments and questions during the conversation?

1	2	3	4	5	6	7	8	9	10

PACE — Does the conversation flow easily or is it awkward with long pauses?

1	2	3	4	5	6	7	8	9	10

OVERALL EFFECT — Is the conversation interesting, informative, and productive?

1	2	3	4	5	6	7	8	9	10

TOTAL SCORE: _____   1 –39 Needs Improvement
40–55 Satisfactory
56–64 Good
65–70 Excellent

COMMENTS: _____
_____
_____
_____

When you were conversing with your partner did you find that there was a time when the conversation stopped? A good conversationalist prevents this from happening by asking questions which will once again get the conversation active. Asking questions also proves that you are interested in what the other person has to say and prevents you from monopolizing the conversation. If someone you are talking with asks you a question, do not simply answer "yes" or "no". A "yes" or "no" response is a real conversation killer. Always try to expand your answer to keep the conversation active.

TAKE ACTION #6

A. With a partner, select a topic which you would like to discuss. Once you have chosen the topic, write four questions to ask your partner. Begin your conversation and include your questions as you talk. Do not simply ask your partner four questions.

B. Compare the questions each of you prepared and how each of you answered them. Were some of the questions answered by "yes" or "no"? Could the answer be expanded or should the question be reworded?

C. Select another topic of conversation. Do not prepare questions ahead of time but ask questions as you talk. Analyse each of the conversations—when you asked questions and when you answered them. Which conversation was the most active and productive— the one with planned questions or the one where questions were not prepared?

D. You are going to conduct an interview with one of your classmates to find out what your classmate thinks about the current television shows. Prepare a list of ten questions on this topic, then select a partner and interview each other. After the interview, write a brief summary of the answers given to your questions.

E. As a class, make a complete list of the questions used above. Select the questions that were the most effective and discuss the reasons for your decision.

F. Your assignment for this evening is to read the feature article in the major daily newspaper of your area (the article that accompanies the headline on page one). Try to expand the information you read by watching the news on television and by listening to the news on the radio. Concentrate on the main story only. During your next class, hold a discussion on the news item. Be prepared to participate by asking questions, contributing information, and expressing your own opinion.

DIFFICULT CONVERSATIONS

Some business conversations may be difficult; for example, asking for a raise or criticizing someone's work. Anticipating and planning for potential problems can make these conversations easier.

For example, there may be times at work when you get upset, angry and frustrated. Your first reaction is to lash out verbally — don't!

Before you argue, think about the consequences and decide what you may gain or lose. With your emotions riding high you may say the wrong things to the wrong person and damage your career.

If you have a legitimate cause for your anger, try to find a solution, then present your case to the right person, at the right time, speaking calmly and rationally.

There are three conditions that should exist before you argue at work:

- The problem should be a permanent one.
  (If the problem is temporary, don't argue. Save yourself for more important matters.)
- The problem should be serious.
  (No one should argue over trivia.)
- You should have a real chance to win.
  (If you can't see a reasonable opportunity to win, then don't argue. It's pointless.)

If all three conditions apply to your situation and you disagree with someone, remember these tips — the art of arguing:

- Try to see the other person's situation before you argue — you can then present your case in a manner more acceptable to that person.
- Present your argument to the person who can solve the problem.

- Don't get personal. Be businesslike and firm, but polite.
- Listen as well as talk.
- Stick to the issue—don't bring up other problems from the past.
- Present at least one possible solution to the problem. This shows that you want to help and are not just complaining.
- Whether you win or lose, accept the final decision graciously.

TAKE ACTION #7
A. Read the following situations.

(i) Employee: "I know you are busy Ms. Hire but I really think that I have the right to ask for a raise. I have a lot of expenses and a raise would be good right now."
Ms. Hire: "You're right, I am busy. Please make an appointment with my secretary. We need time to discuss this matter properly."

(ii) Manager: "I want you to redo this work you gave me yesterday. It is not what I want at all—full of mistakes and messy. Have it ready by five o'clock."
Employee: "But I have this rush assignment to do first! What mistakes did I make? I followed the instructions you gave me."

(iii) Fellow employee: "I heard that you are in serious trouble because you're always late and taking days off. You'd better smarten up."
Employee: "Mind your own business!"

B. How would you handle each situation?

(i) Make a list of the points you would want to mention during your conversation with Ms. Hire. With a partner, write a new dialogue asking Ms. Hire for a raise.

(ii) If you were not pleased with someone's work, how would you tell them? If someone criticized your work, how would you react? With a partner, write a new dialogue between the manager and the employee.

(iii) With your partner, discuss how you would help a fellow employee in a positive manner if you were aware that their behaviour was not acceptable. How would you react to someone who was trying to help you?

C. As a class, discuss how anticipating and planning for potential problems might have helped in each of the three sample situations. Using the list of tips for arguing on p. 153 as a model, make a list of hints for handling difficult conversations.

ENDING CONVERSATIONS

The way you end a conversation is just as important as the way you begin it. The ending leaves the other person with a lasting impression. It is best that that impression be a good one. For example, what would your impression be of someone who ended a business conversation with "Thanks, that'd be great" or "I'll get back to you when I get a chance"?

TAKE ACTION #8

A. As a class, discuss how you can make a good impression when you end a conversation. Make a list of any hints or tips that might help you.

Television and radio interviewers are professional questioners. They are paid to keep the conversation active, interesting, and informative.

TAKE ACTION #9

A. Your teacher will bring in tapes and videos of both radio and television interviewers. Make notes on the three stages of the interview: the beginning, the middle (sustaining the conversation), and the end. Listen very carefully to how the interviewer questions to sustain the interview and what the responses are. Play the videotapes again and watch the body language, the appearance, and distance of the two people participating in the interview. Discuss as a class which interviewer was the most effective and why. (See copyright notice on p. ix .)

PRESENTATIONS

There will be occasions in business when you will have to talk in a formal manner to more than one or two people. It could be that you have an idea for a new procedure to be used in the company or you might have to make a sales presentation. Whatever the reason, you will have to plan what you will say and how you will say it, then make a presentation.

TAKE ACTION #10

A. Your teacher will bring a grab-bag of goodies to class. You will recognize the items. Each student in your class will reach in the bag and retrieve an item. You will have three minutes to plan how you will describe the item's function to the class. You can be serious or humorous. The function can be real or imagined. You should be prepared to speak for a minimum of two minutes and a maximum of four.

B. As a class, list the factors that contribute to an effective presentation. Make a second list of the factors that contribute to a poor presentation.

FORMAL PRESENTATIONS

When you plan a formal presentation there should be a beginning, a middle, and a conclusion. For the beginning or conclusion, you could ask a question, use an anecdote or quotation, reveal your purpose, or issue a challenge. An example of an introduction that grabs the audience's attention is this:

"Are you ready for five different careers, working for thirty years, and fulfilling several other roles at the same time? Well, start getting ready. Statistics show that this is your future!" (The speaker then continues by discussing long-term goal planning and job search techniques.)

To provide a good initial impression and a sound conclusion, you may want to memorize the beginning and end of your speech. However, the major part of your material should not be memorized. Reciting from memory sometimes sounds artificial and you can forget your speech under stress. Instead of memorizing, know your topic thoroughly and write on cards the points you wish to cover. Using notes will help you be relaxed and natural.

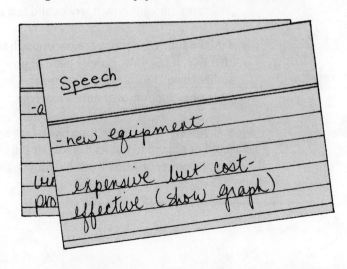

TAKE ACTION #11

A. Prepare a presentation based on an interview with someone you have known since you were a young child; e.g., a parent or grandparent or a family friend. The purpose of the interview is to find out some incident from your past which would be interesting to tell the class. Your presentation should be five minutes long and may be serious or humorous. When you are preparing at home, practise with a tape recorder or in front of a mirror.

B. Working in groups of three, make your presentations. As one person makes a presentation, the other two should observe and analyse it using a copy of the checklist on p. 161. When you have finished, discuss your evaluations and suggest any improvements that each of you could make.

PROPS

Many business presentations involve the use of props, such as a product, audio-visual equipment, a chart, or a picture. Using props can add interest to your presentation and make it more effective. Used improperly, however, they can detract from your performance. Here are a few tips to help you use props effectively:

• Decide which props would help you the most. For example it would be more effective to use a pie graph showing a company's division of profits than to give a list of figures during a speech. Use props that will help you explain things or get your point across but don't use too many—they're supposed to help you, not replace your speech.

• Practise using your props ahead of time. If you will be using unfamiliar equipment (such as an audio system or an overhead projector), find out how it works and test it before your presentation.

• Make sure your props are big enough to be seen and be effective. If possible, check ahead of time to ensure that the audience will be able to see properly. Check sound quality, too, if your presentation uses audio material.

• If you are using something like a large chart, have it put on a stand or affixed to the wall. This not only looks more professional, it will save your arms from becoming tired!

• Highlight your prop only when you are using it to illustrate a point. When you need it, show it—turn to it, point to it, or hold it up to the audience if it's small. Before and after you use it, keep it away from the audience's attention — it can be distracting.

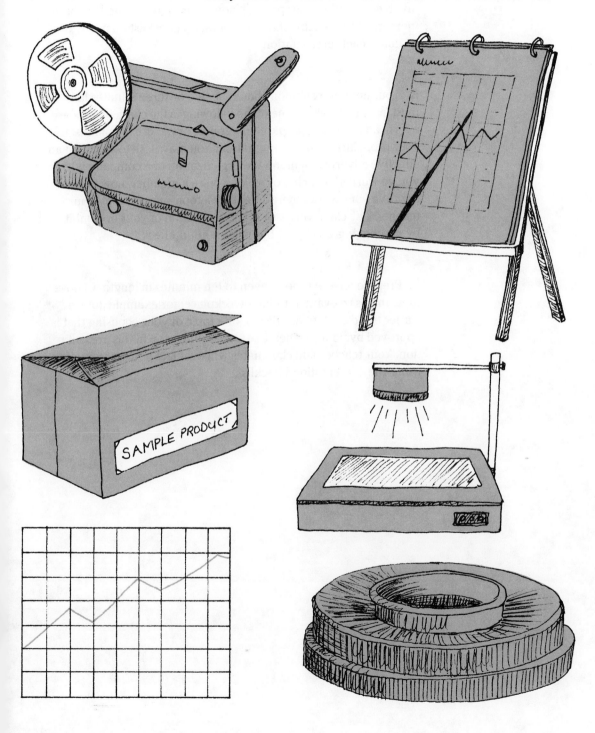

TAKE ACTION #12

A. Using a prop give a one-minute presentation telling the class how to perform a task; for example, how to pot a plant, ski, tie a tie, juggle, or a topic you clear with your teacher. Think out the steps involved and plan your props. Know your material and try not to memorize! Use a copy of the presentation checklist on p. 161 to evaluate each presentation.

B. Your next presentation should be two or three minutes long and must include the use of one of the following: a flip chart, blackboard, overhead projector, prepared diagrams, or pictures. You must use your prop during your presentation. You may wish to speak on an effective advertisement, on the organization of a company where you've worked or a club of which you're a member, how to improve your work environment, or a topic approved by your teacher. The class will assist in the evaluation of your presentation by completing a copy of the presentation checklist.

C. Prepare an oral report seven to ten minutes in length. Choose a topic that is relevant to today's workplace; for example, future career trends, safety on the job, or a topic of your choosing that is approved by your teacher. Use at least one prop in this presentation. Your teacher and classmates will evaluate your presentation using the presentation checklist.

PRESENTATION CHECKLIST

Rate each component on a scale from 1 (Needs Improvement) to 10 (Excellent)—a rating of 6 would mean Satisfactory. Add up your ratings to find your total score.

VOICE CONTROL — Rate the intonation, pitch, volume, pace, clarity, and voice quality.

| 1 | 2 | 3 | 4 | 5 | 6 | 7 | 8 | 9 | 10 |

APPEARANCE — Is the speaker well-groomed and business-like?

| 1 | 2 | 3 | 4 | 5 | 6 | 7 | 8 | 9 | 10 |

BODY LANGUAGE — Is the speaker's body language effective?

| 1 | 2 | 3 | 4 | 5 | 6 | 7 | 8 | 9 | 10 |

USE OF PROPS — Are the props appropriate, used with ease, and a positive addition?

| 1 | 2 | 3 | 4 | 5 | 6 | 7 | 8 | 9 | 10 |

CONTENT

Opening — Is it effective and interesting?

| 1 | 2 | 3 | 4 | 5 | 6 | 7 | 8 | 9 | 10 |

Subject Matter — Is the material interesting, suitable, accurate, and complete?

| 1 | 2 | 3 | 4 | 5 | 6 | 7 | 8 | 9 | 10 |

Level of Language — Is it too technical, too formal or informal, or appropriate?

| 1 | 2 | 3 | 4 | 5 | 6 | 7 | 8 | 9 | 10 |

Length of Presentation — Is the report concise and complete?

| 1 | 2 | 3 | 4 | 5 | 6 | 7 | 8 | 9 | 10 |

Conclusion — Is it brief, a good summary of the speech, and a positive ending?

| 1 | 2 | 3 | 4 | 5 | 6 | 7 | 8 | 9 | 10 |

TOTAL SCORE: _____

1 –49 Needs Improvement
50–64 Satisfactory
65–79 Good
80–90 Excellent

COMMENTS: _____
_____
_____
_____

TAKE ACTION #13

A. Invite someone who is in a career which depends on good communication skills to come to your class to give a presentation and be interviewed; for example, a politician, union leader, or salesperson. As a class,

(i) Choose the speaker and date of the presentation.

(ii) Compose an invitation to be given by mail or by telephone.

(iii) Make a list of questions you will ask.

(iv) Divide the following responsibilities among your classmates:
- introducing the guest speaker
- making notes and summarizing the speech
- asking the selected questions
- making notes and summarizing the answers
- thanking the guest speaker.

(v) After the guest speaker leaves, fill out a presentation checklist for future reference.

(vi) Compose a letter thanking the guest speaker.

B. In your next class, compare the checklists you filled out earlier. Discuss what parts of the presentation were done effectively and what improvements, if any, could be made.

JOB SEARCH III

Getting Ready

You have decided what type of career you would like to pursue; you know where to look for job leads. Now it is time to get ready and apply for those jobs.

RESUMES

A résumé is something you will use for virtually every job application. You can mail it or give it to prospective employers or use it to help you answer questions quickly and easily when you apply for a job by phone.

Your résumé is an important summary of facts which will assist you in selling your accomplishments and qualities to a future employer. It will include much of the basic information from your personal data sheet (see p. 131).

Your résumé should be no more than one or two pages long. If your résumé is longer than that, a prospective employer might be too busy to spend time reading it. More in-depth information can be given during the job interview.

There are several different ways of organizing your résumé depending on the type and amount of work experience you have. Two particular styles of résumé are outlined on the following pages. Note that while the arrangement of information is different, the basic facts provided are the same in each. This is true of all résumés. Your résumé should include:

- **Personal Information** (name, address, phone number)

- **Education** (secondary and, where applicable, post-secondary)

- **Skills** (typing, computer programming, arc welding, word processing, report writing, etc.)

- **Achievements** (diplomas, trophies, prizes)

- **Work Experience** (volunteer work, babysitting, paper route, part-time jobs, summer jobs, school work programs, co-operative education — mention any promotions you received)

- **Outside Interests** (track team, debating club, jazz dancing, piano playing, etc.)

- **References** (teachers, former employers, clergy, youth club/organization leaders, etc., but not a relative — ask before you list people as references)

A résumé demonstrates to an employer that you are organized, prepared, and serious about seeking a job. Make sure it is typed on good quality paper, error-free, and up to date. Make photocopies only if the copies are of excellent quality.

Chronological Arrangement

RESUME

LISA MARIE BEAUCHAMPS

Address:	1735 New Street Halifax, Nova Scotia B3J 2V9
Telephone:	(902) 555-5678
Education:	Grade 12 graduate, 1986 Grey Owl High School, Halifax
Skills:	Typing — 40 wpm Shorthand — 100 wpm CPR Instructor's Certificate
Work Experience:	1985 Receptionist during the summer. Antique Automobile Appraisals, 345 Tusek Trail, Pagetown, Ontario M1W 1K3
	1984 Cashier part-time after school. Flair Fashions Ltd. 33 David Drive, Halifax, Nova Scotia B3K 2S9
	1983 Babysitting. Mrs. Susan Hathaway, Suite 101, 900 Shirley Circle, Halifax, Nova Scotia B3M 1A8
References:	Upon Request

Biographical Arrangement

MARY MITCHELL

800 Front Street   (416) 555-1234   Uxbridge, Ontario   LOC 1A0

EDUCATION
Orchard Park High School, Scarborough, Ontario
Uxbridge Collegiate Institute, Uxbridge, Ontario

ACHIEVEMENTS AND OUTSIDE INTERESTS
Manager, school track team
Dagmar ski team
Member of 4H Club
School attendance award, 1985

WORK EXPERIENCE
Volunteer work for Uxbridge Cottage Hospital
Camp Counsellor — YWCA Day Camp
Homan's Shoe Store — co-operative education placement as
salesperson and stock clerk

SKILLS
Cashiering	Answering the telephone
Pricing	Organizing shelves and displays
Inventory	Dealing with customers

REFERENCES
Mrs. M. Saunders	Mr. J. Clarke
E & S Well Drilling,	Science Teacher,
General Delivery,	Uxbridge Collegiate Institute,
Greenbank, Ontario	Uxbridge, Ontario
LOG 5Y8	LOC 7J4
(555-6789)	(555-2345)

Dr. I. Taylor
Uxbridge Cottage Hospital,
Uxbridge, Ontario
LOK 6R7
(555-4567)

GETTING DOWN TO BUSINESS #1
A. (i) Using your personal data sheet (p. 131) and your job skills list from Job Search I (p. 34), write a rough draft of your résumé.

(ii) Work with a partner to suggest improvement in each other's résumé.

B. Prepare the final, edited version of your résumé. Proofread it carefully before placing it in your Job Search Kit.

LETTERS OF APPLICATION
Whenever you send your résumé to someone, it should be accompanied by a letter of application. Whether you are responding to a specific job advertisement or inquiring about job opportunities at a company, your letter should be concise yet contain enough information to impress a prospective employer with your qualifications and potential.

When you are answering an advertisement, make sure that you include all the information requested. Do not repeat what is in your résumé but try to mention at least two qualifications that would be valuable for that job. Unless the ad says otherwise, always type your letter of application.

For example, the following letter of application was written in response to this advertisement:

Wanted — Assistant Mechanic. Exp. helpful but not nec. Good entry position. Reply with résumé and references to Mr. Murray Hull, Hull and Macklin's Garage, Cold Lake.

<table>
<tr><td>

Your
Address ⟶

</td><td>

29 Main Street
Grand Centre, Alberta
TOC 2B5
May 10, 19__

</td></tr>
</table>

29 Main Street
Grand Centre, Alberta
TOC 2B5
May 10, 19__

Mr. Murray Hull
Hull and Macklin's Garage
Cold Lake, Alberta
TOA 1AO

Dear Mr. Hull:

How you heard about the job / Intent to Apply ⟶
    While reading the Cold Lake Tribune this morning, I read your advertisement for an assistant mechanic. I would like to apply for that job.

Qualifications ⟶
    For the past four years, I have taken courses in auto mechanics in school. Since I was thirteen, I have helped my uncle in his garage here in Cold Lake. I did most of the tune-up work for him last summer. Two months ago he sold his garage and retired.

References ⟶
Résumé Mentioned ⟶
    If you need references, you may contact my auto mechanics teacher, Ms. Linda Winder, or my former employer, Ms. Barb Forrest. Their addresses are included in my résumé which I have enclosed with this letter.

Request for Interview ⟶
How to Contact You ⟶
    I shall graduate from Grand Centre High School on June 15. After that I shall be ready to go to work. I can come to your garage for an interview when it is convenient for you. You can write me at the above address or call me at my home. My phone number is (403) 555-1234.

Yours truly,

Lisa L'Amoreaux

Lisa L'Amoreaux

Alert the receiver to your enclosed résumé ⟶
Enclosure

When you write more general letters to companies which have not advertised any positions, state the kind of job you're looking for and your qualifications. (See the example on p. 170.) Whenever possible, phone the company to find out the correct name, spelling, and title of the person to whom you should address your letter. Use the checklist on p. 108 to help you make your job application letters effective.

GETTING DOWN TO BUSINESS #2

A. Using a recent help wanted ad for a job in which you're interested, write a letter of application to accompany your résumé.

B. Referring to the list of leads you compiled in Job Search II (p. 58), choose one of the companies you've identified and prepare a general letter of application asking if there are any jobs available. You may have to phone the company to obtain the correct mailing address and the name of the person to whom you should write.

490 Grayson Road
Ottawa, Ontario
K1P 9V8
February 13, 19__

J. K. Wilson Company
Commercial Photographers
98 Lambert Lane
Burlington, Ontario
L7L 2C4

Dear Mr. Wilson

I am greatly interested in obtaining a position with your company.

As you will see from the enclosed résumé, I have considerable
background in the field of photography. I have worked as a
photographer's assistant in summer jobs and have also taken many
courses in this subject.

I would appreciate the opportunity to meet you and discuss the
possibilities of employment with your firm. I shall call you in a few
days to see whether an interview can be arranged.

Yours sincerely

James R. Chan

James R. Chan

Enclosure

TELEPHONING FOR AN INTERVIEW

Sometimes using the telephone is the most efficient way to find out if there are jobs available at a number of companies. Also, some help wanted ads will tell you to apply by calling the company. The objective is still the same as when you apply in writing—you would like to be granted a personal interview. Therefore, careful planning before you call is essential. If you do not plan well, it might cost you a job.

Before you call:

- have your résumé and personal data sheet at hand so that you can answer questions quickly and accurately.
- have a notepad and a pen or pencil ready.
- make a list of questions you want to ask.
- have a list of times and days that you are available for interviews.
- have the name of the person to whom you should speak (if it is given in an ad).
- practise what you are going to say.

When you call:

- place your call between 9:00 and 11:00 in the morning or between 2:00 and 4:00 in the afternoon.
- speak clearly and slowly.
- state why you are calling.
- listen carefully to the other person.
- answer questions briefly, positively, and enthusiastically.
- ask questions if you need to know more about the job advertised or what kinds of jobs might be available.
- make notes during the call.
- request an interview.
- write the time, date, location, and name of the person to see if you are granted an interview.
- if you are calling to inquire about job opportunities and there are no positions available, ask if there might be any openings in the near future and if you could send in your résumé to be kept on file.

GETTING DOWN TO BUSINESS #3

A. Working in groups of three, take turns role-playing telephone calls to apply for jobs. Each of you will make two phone calls. The first phone call will be in answer to a help wanted ad from a recent newspaper. The second phone call will be to one of the companies you identified in your list of leads from Job Search II (p. 58). In each case, one person will be the job applicant, one will do the interviewing, and the other will use a copy of the telephone interview checklist (p. 173) for evaluation. After each phone call, use the checklist to discuss how effective the conversation was and how it might be improved.

B. As a class, make a list of tips for telephone interviews and keep a copy of it with a copy of the checklist in your Job Search Kit.

C. Write a script for one of the telephone conversations you had and give it to your teacher for evaluation.

TELEPHONE INTERVIEW CHECKLIST

Date:

Company: Phone:

Contact Person: Title:

	Yes	No
Did you make sure you were prepared before you called?	☐	☐
Did you know what you wanted to say?	☐	☐
Did you introduce yourself properly?	☐	☐
Did you state your reason for calling?	☐	☐
Did you sound enthusiastic and positive about the job?	☐	☐
Did you ask questions if you needed more information about the job?	☐	☐
Did you outline your qualifications?	☐	☐
Did you make notes of important points?	☐	☐
Did you request an interview and/or ask if you could send a copy of your résumé?	☐	☐
Did you speak clearly and slowly?	☐	☐

General Comments:

_____

_____

If interview granted,

Time:
Date:
Location:
Interviewer:
Directions:

APPLYING IN PERSON

Sometimes an advertisement will ask you to apply in person. You may also decide that making a "cold call" is the best way to follow up some job leads. Whatever your reason for applying for a job in person, there are several guidelines you should follow:

- Plan what you will say before you go.
- Dress appropriately and go alone.
- Take at least one copy of your résumé to leave at the company and a copy of your personal data sheet to help you fill out application forms.
- Take paper and several pens.
- If you are answering an ad, make a note of the name of the person you should see.
- If you are making a cold call where no jobs have been advertised, ask for the name of the person responsible for hiring. If that person isn't in, or if there are no openings, ask if you can leave your résumé or fill out an application form. Make a note to follow up with another visit or a phone call or letter.
- Be polite to everyone you meet—they could be future colleagues and may have some input into who is hired. Sometimes companies use their receptionists as the first step in the screening process.

APPLICATION FORMS

Many more application forms are completed by job seekers than letters of application are written or personal interviews conducted. It is the most frequently used tool of the employer in identifying the successful job applicant. Employers find it easier to compare job applicants if all the information is in the same format for each person.

When you are filling out an application form, remember the following:

- Be neat—a busy employer may reject an application form on appearance alone. If the application form instructs you to print, do so. Print legibly and do not fold or wrinkle the form. If you do make a mistake, cross it out neatly and put in the correct information.
- Use your personal data sheet and your résumé to help you fill out the form quickly and accurately.

- Be complete—answer all questions. If a question is not applicable, write N/A in the space. This tells the employer that you did not overlook the question.
- When you have finished, check to make sure that you have answered all the questions, that your answers make sense, and that you have signed your name.

GETTING DOWN TO BUSINESS #4

A. Read the sample application form (pp. 176-177). Using your personal data sheet and your résumé, fill out the copy of this form that your teacher gives you. As a class, discuss any questions or problems you may have filling out application forms.

APPLICATION FOR EMPLOYMENT

Position being applied for	Date available to begin work

PERSONAL DATA

Last name	Given name(s)	Social Insurance Number
		_ _

Address	Street	Apt. No.	Home Telephone Number

City	Province	Postal Code	Business Telephone No.

Please indicate how you want to be addressed in any correspondence.   □ As above   □ Mr   □ Mrs   □ Miss   □ Ms

Are you willing to re-locate? □ Yes □ No	Preferred location	Do you have a valid driver's licence? □ Yes □ No	Class

To determine your qualification for employment, please provide below and on the reverse, information related to your academic and other achievements including voluntary work, as well as employment history. Additional information may be attached on a separate sheet.

EDUCATION

SECONDARY SCHOOL		BUSINESS, TRADE, OR TECHNICAL SCHOOL	
Highest grade or level completed		Name of course	Length of course
Type of certificate or diploma received		Licence, certificate, or diploma awarded? □ Yes □ No	

COMMUNITY COLLEGE		UNIVERSITY		
Name of Program	Length of Program	Length of course	Degree awarded □ Yes □ No	□ Pass □ Honours
Diploma received? □ Yes □ No		Major subject		
Other courses, workshops, seminars		Licences, Certificates, Degrees		

Work-related skills

Describe any of your work-related skills, experience, or training that relate to the position for which you are applying.

EMPLOYMENT

Name and Address of present/last employer.	Present/Last job title	
	Period of employment From To	Present/Last salary
	Name of Supervisor	Telephone
Type of Business	Reason for leaving	

Duties/Responsibilities

Name and Address of previous employer.	Previous job title	
	Period of employment From To	Final salary
	Name of Supervisor	Telephone
Type of Business	Reason for leaving	

Duties/Responsibilities

Name and Address of previous employer.	Previous job title	
	Period of employment From To	Final salary
	Name of Supervisor	Telephone
Type of Business	Reason for leaving	

Duties/Responsibilities

For employment references, may we approach:
Your present/last employer?   ☐ Yes   ☐ No
Your former employer(s)?   ☐ Yes   ☐ No

List references if different than above on a separate sheet.

Activities (civic, athletic, etc.)

I hereby declare that the preceding information
is true and complete to my knowledge.
I understand that a false statement may
disqualify me from employment, or
cause my dismissal.

_____   _____
Signature   Date

THE BUSINESS OF MEETINGS

7

I like meetings.
ANONYMOUS

> ## TAKE NOTE
> Meetings are held for two reasons — to share information and to make decisions.

Meetings are an important and necessary part of your life — both personal and professional. Even if you do not attend any formal business meetings, you participate in many informal meetings. For example, you attend meetings of clubs or organizations to which you belong; you may hold informal meetings with your friends to decide your plans for the weekend; and you have probably held meetings with your fellow students to discuss and work on group activities in this class.

TAKE ACTION #1
A. As a class make a list of the various meetings in which you have participated recently. Identify the purpose(s) of each meeting.

BUSINESS MEETINGS
Some business meetings are held because the law requires that they are, others for convenience or necessity. They can range from an informal gathering of two or more people who might meet casually once a week to discuss production schedules, to a very formal Annual General Meeting which concerns the actions of a large corporation and could include hundreds of people.

There are many advantages to holding business meetings, the most obvious being that there are many people providing information and different viewpoints to problems. Feedback is immediate, and input from all those attending helps to ensure that the best interests of the whole group are being considered. Also, when people feel they are involved in the decision-making process, it improves morale and helps them accept decisions more readily.

Meetings vary greatly in size and formality; for example, from a spontaneous and casual meeting in an office hallway to a carefully planned and structured departmental meeting.

Sometimes, though, decisions are delayed by waiting until meetings are arranged to deal with them. Further delays can be caused when no decision is reached at the meeting, and the matter is referred to a committee or is held back to be studied more carefully. Another disadvantage is that while people are organizing and attending meetings, their daily work in the company is not being done. Meetings are expensive when they involve renting facilities, serving refreshments, and reimbursing out-of-town participants for accommodation and travel expenses. Meetings cost money, so it is important that they be as productive and efficient as possible.

TAKE ACTION #2
A. Refer to the meetings you listed in Take Action #1. As a class, discuss how productive each of these meetings was and why.

TAKE NOTE
Whether formal or informal, large or small, successful meetings have several things in common:

- Everyone who attends understands the purpose of the meeting and has the information necessary to participate effectively.
- Everyone who attends will benefit from or be able to contribute to the meeting.
- Someone who is competent and fair directs the meeting or leads the discussion.

These are all important requirements for a productive and efficient meeting, but how they are met will vary depending on the size and formality of the meeting. For example, in a very formal meeting, the purpose may be stated in a published notice of meeting and the business to be discussed will be listed on an agenda which is distributed to participants by registered mail. For an informal meeting, you may receive a memo that says your department will be having a meeting to discuss the budget. For an even more informal meeting, your boss may simply come to your office to talk to you and your co-workers about a problem.

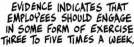

In a formal business setting, the meeting is directed by a chairperson who has very clearly defined duties and responsibilities. In a departmental meeting, the head of the department usually assumes the role of chairperson to lead the discussion. In the third example above, your boss may direct the conversation, or it may be led by the person who is most familiar with the problem. In this meeting the discussion is likely to be more casual and spontaneous.

FORMAL BUSINESS MEETINGS

Formal meetings are conducted according to strict rules of order which are based on parliamentary procedure. Under these rules, the rights and responsibilities of the participants are very clearly established, as are the ways in which the meeting is run. While any company or organization may have its own constitution or by-laws, the following are the basic guidelines for conducting formal meetings.

THE CHAIRPERSON

A competent chairperson is perhaps the most important factor in a successful meeting. Referred to in the third person as "the chair," she or he presides over the meeting and is responsible for ensuring that it is conducted properly, fairly, and efficiently. The chairperson:

- is responsible for knowing and enforcing the rules for a meeting.
- establishes that everything is in order and declares the meeting open.
- announces in turn the items to be considered at the meeting, following the agenda that has been previously set.

- directs the discussion of each item by ensuring that everyone gets a chance to speak and that the discussion stays on topic.
- puts each item to a vote when necessary, counts the votes, and announces the result.
- signs the minutes or record of what happened at the meeting to show she or he agrees with them.
- cannot propose or second a motion or proposal.

THE SECRETARY

The secretary, sometimes called the recording secretary, is responsible for the records of the committee, company, or department and the records of its meetings. The secretary:

- keeps a record of the rules the organization, company, or department uses for meetings and notes any changes that are made to them.
- keeps a register of members.
- sends out notices of meetings.
- prepares an agenda or list of items of business to be considered at the meeting.
- makes the arrangements for a meeting room, seating, refreshments, and any materials that may be needed (such as writing materials or audio-visual equipment).
- is responsible for the minutes or official record of a meeting.
  — reads the minutes or proceedings of the previous meeting
  — makes note of what was said and done at the meeting and types up the minutes
  — signs the minutes (with the chairperson) to indicate that she or he agrees with them.

THE TREASURER

The duties of the treasurer vary from group to group and, in small organizations, are sometimes combined with those of the secretary. The treasurer looks after the finances of the group that is meeting, not necessarily the finances of the entire company. She or he:

- keeps a record of the money of the committee or organization and pays the bills when directed.
- is responsible for making financial reports annually and sometimes quarterly.

NOTICE OF MEETING

For formal meetings a notice of meeting must be sent to everyone concerned. In order to be valid, this notice must state the purpose of the meeting as well as the date, time, and place. It also must be signed by the proper authority which varies depending on who is holding the meeting.

J & S
Manufacturing Limited
Notice of Meeting of Directors

Take notice that a meeting of the board of directors of J & S Manufacturing Limited will be held at the Head Office, the 23rd day of September at the hour of 9 a.m. The agenda is attached.

Dated _____

By order of the Chief Executive Officer

_____
(Secretary)

OPENING THE MEETING

The chairperson opens a meeting or *calls a meeting to order*. First it is noted that the chairperson, secretary, and treasurer are present. Then it must be established that there is a *quorum*. A quorum is the minimum number of qualified people who are required to attend a meeting so that business may be legally conducted. Unless there is a specific number stated in the rules, a quorum is a simple majority (fifty-one per cent) of the members of the committee. If there is not a quorum present, the meeting must be adjourned. (Anyone may also demand that the chairperson make a quorum count at any time during the meeting to make sure there are enough people present.) Once these requirements have been met, the chairperson declares the meeting open.

AGENDA

A meeting must follow the agenda or order of business prepared by the secretary prior to the meeting. The agenda follows a specific order. First the minutes or record of what happened at the previous meeting are read. This is followed by reports that the group has requested from boards and committees, unfinished business from previous meetings, and finally by new business.

AGENDA

Sales & Marketing Department
Monthly Meeting

Date: 19__ 03 13
Place: Conference Room
Time: 9:30 a.m.

1. Reading of the minutes from the February meeting.
2. New equipment purchase proposal — Beverly Bettens
3. Report on the National Computer Conference — Earl Sauder
4. Sales Summary — Paul Dion
5. New Business

MOTIONS

A motion is a proposal to do or discuss something. In fact, no item of business may be discussed or decided at a formal meeting without a motion to do so. For example, if you wish to open discussion on a report, you might say, "I move that we accept the report of the finance committee."

Each motion must be seconded by someone else. Seconding a motion does not necessarily show approval of a proposal—it merely indicates you think the matter should be discussed. It is possible, though not usual, to second a motion and vote against it later.

Only when a motion has been proposed and seconded may discussion begin. Every member has the right to speak once on each motion. It is the chairperson's responsibility to ensure that discussion is fair but does not waste time or wander off the topic.

If someone wants to delay discussion of an issue, there are several ways of *tabling* or *deferring a motion*. A *motion to adjourn discussion* states the time that the discussion of the matter will resume. A *motion to postpone indefinitely* doesn't state a specific time to resume discussion, but the motion may be renewed at any future meeting. A motion may also be made to *refer* an issue to a committee or board for further study.

Unless a motion is tabled, discussion continues until an amendment is proposed or a vote is taken (see Figure 7.1).

AMENDMENTS

While a motion is "on the floor" or being discussed, it may be amended or changed by another motion. The amendment has the same requirements as a main motion—it must be moved and seconded before it can be discussed and voted on. The people who proposed and seconded the first motion may not propose or second an amendment to it.

Once an amendment has been moved and seconded, no one can discuss the original motion until they have voted on the amendment. If the amendment is defeated, the discussion returns to the original motion. If the amendment is passed, the original motion is changed and discussion of the newly-worded motion begins (see Figure 7.2).

VOTING

When everyone has finished discussing a motion, the chairperson re-states the motion and calls for a vote. At other times, someone may move to *close discussion* which means that a vote has to be taken immediately. This is also referred to as *calling*, *closing*, or *putting the question*. The chairperson may reject this motion if she or he decides that there should be more discussion before the vote.

If a motion to call the question is accepted and seconded, everyone must vote immediately. They do not vote on the original motion; they decide if there has been enough discussion on the original motion. If the motion to call the question is passed, it means they can't discuss the original motion any more but must vote on it. If the motion to call the question is defeated, they may continue discussing the original motion (see Figure 7.3).

Most ordinary questions are decided by a simple majority (fifty-one per cent of the votes) but some require a larger majority (e.g., two-thirds of the votes). Voting is usually done by a voice vote, a show of hands, or by ballot. If the results using a voice or show of hands vote are unclear, anyone who voted may ask for a poll or vote by ballot to be taken. This method must also be used if anything has to be decided by more than a simple majority.

In company meetings, there is no such thing as a secret vote— even when a poll is taken, each voter must write her or his name on the ballot. The chairperson is responsible for deciding the results of a voice or show of hands vote. If a poll is taken, it is also the chairperson who collects, examines, and counts the ballots and announces the result.

If a motion is carried or passed, it becomes a resolution. When a motion is defeated or is not passed, it is said that the resolution is lost. Where a simple majority is required, and the vote is tied, the motion is not passed.

POINTS OF ORDER

Anyone at a meeting may make a *point of order*, demanding that the rules be followed or indicating that there has been a violation of the rules. For example, if an amendment has been moved and seconded, and someone begins to discuss the original motion, a point of order, indicating this and asking that the chairperson direct the discussion back to the amendment, could be made.

Once someone has demanded a point of order, the meeting stops until the matter has been decided. The chairperson's ruling is final—if the point is accepted, the situation is corrected; if it is rejected, the chairperson resumes the meeting. In the example above, the chairperson would probably accept the point of order and restrict discussion to the amendment.

Other examples of when a point of order demand could be made are if someone speaks out of turn, if someone speaks more than once on the same motion, or if the person who proposed a motion also proposes an amendment to it.

CLOSING THE MEETING

There are different kinds of motions to finish a meeting. A *motion to adjourn to a fixed day* means that when the meeting resumes, the agenda of the original meeting will continue and no new business will be added. A *motion to conclude* or *terminate the meeting* means the meeting is dissolved and all unfinished business is cancelled. As with other motions, a motion to adjourn and a motion to conclude the meeting must be seconded and voted on.

Some less formal motions for closing a meeting.

MINUTES OF THE MEETING

After a meeting a form of business report called the minutes is prepared by the recording secretary. The minutes are the official record of the meeting and include:

- the name of the group and the purpose of the meeting
- the date, time, and place of the meeting
- the names of the chairperson, secretary, and treasurer
- the names of all those present, and apologies received from those who could not attend
- whether the minutes of the previous meeting were read and approved

- a record of what resolutions were passed, what appointments were made, and what business was conducted
- the hours of the meeting and adjournment

The minutes are usually signed by the chairperson and the secretary and are read and approved at the next meeting. They usually contain only a record of what happened at a meeting, not what was said by the speakers. They never include any comment, favourable or otherwise, on what was said or done at a meeting.

J & S
Manufacturing Limited
Sales & Marketing Department

Minutes of Meeting of 19__ 03 13

Attendance	All members were present.
Minutes	The minutes of the meeting of February 1, 19__ were read and approved.
New Equipment Purchases	Beverly Betten reported that the department is in good shape regarding equipment. Her report on projected equipment needs was accepted and it was decided that $8,000 would be budgeted for a word processor to be purchased by the end of the year. Beverly is to research various systems and give her recommendations as to which should be purchased at the next meeting.
Computer Conference	Earl Sauder reported on the variety of seminars offered at the conference. He thought the conference was well run and informative. It was decided that at least one member of the department should attend each year.
Monthly Sales	Ten new accounts were added this past month and sales are up fifteen per cent over this month last year. Setting the budget for promotion was tabled because of a delay in getting quotes from the printer.
New Business	Valerie Tralka mentioned that many of the staff members are concerned about the health hazards from secondhand smoke in the office. It was decided that smoking will not be allowed in the sales office, effective immediately.
Adjournment	The meeting adjourned at 11:15.

_____
Chairperson

_____
Secretary

TAKE ACTION #3

A. *Robert's Rules of Order* (Toronto: Checkerbooks Inc., 1981) is the most widely known authority on how to conduct meetings according to parliamentary procedure. Other books, such as *Wainberg's Company Meetings* (Toronto: Canada Law Book Limited, 1969), apply these rules specifically to business meetings. Using *Robert's Rules of Order* and at least one other source, write brief, point-form notes to define the following terms:

- voting by acquiescence
- standing committees and special committees or task forces
- dividing a motion
- voting by proxy
- recognizing a speaker/giving a speaker the floor

B. Working in small groups, attend a meeting held by your town or city council, the Board of Education, your student council, or a club or organization to which you belong. Observe how the meeting is conducted and write a brief report outlining:

- the purpose of the meeting
- who attended
- how frequently they meet
- how formal the meeting was
- the major points discussed and decided

C. Have each group read its report to the class. As a class, compare the meetings you attended. How effective were they? Are there any ways in which they might have been improved? Did the level of formality help or hinder the productivity of the meeting?

INFORMAL BUSINESS MEETINGS

Informal meetings do not have rules that are clearly defined and recorded. The size and nature of the meeting as well as the people who attend will determine the level of formality, but even the most informal meetings follow the same general guidelines as formal meetings.

For example, every meeting needs someone to act as chairperson, even if the person is not referred to by that title. Someone must take charge of the meeting to ensure that it is efficient and fair.

As in formal meetings, everyone concerned should be notified of the meeting and its purpose, and there should be an agenda, written or verbal, listing what is to be discussed and decided at the meeting. Everyone should have a chance to ask questions and express opinions and to see how and why decisions are made. No one should be allowed to waste time with irrelevant or repetitive discussion.

Important decisions are often put to a vote, although sometimes they are only discussed. For example, a supervisor may want to find out how the staff feels about an issue before making a decision. Other issues may be tabled; for example, your boss may ask you to find out more information about a certain matter so that it can be discussed at the next meeting.

It is also good practice to have someone take notes of what was said and done and to give a copy of the notes or minutes to each person who attended. This way everyone has a record of what decisions were made and when.

Most meetings follow the same general guidelines, although the level of formality may differ.

TAKE ACTION #4

A. Put all the skills you have developed (speaking, making a presentation, listening and taking notes, and writing) to use by holding your own fundraising meeting.

Divide the class into groups of five to ten people. For each group, appoint or elect a chairperson and a secretary/treasurer. As a group, decide how formal your meeting(s) will be.

Choose someone to make the arrangements for when and where the meeting will be held and for notifying everyone. Set an agenda for the first meeting and have the secretary type it up and distribute copies to everyone. Your agenda should include discussions on what fundraising activity you will use and where you will donate the money.

Your group may be able to decide everything in one meeting or it may take several meetings to find all the information you need. For example, your group may come up with several methods of raising funds and realize you need more information on how costly each method would be and how much money each would raise, or there may be some disagreement about where the money is needed most. If you have several meetings, take turns being chairperson and secretary.

During the meeting(s) the secretary should take notes of what happens. If another meeting is required, make arrangements and set an agenda for it. After the meeting(s) appoint someone to type up the minutes from the secretary's notes and someone to type up the agenda and give copies to everyone.

When you have made your final decisions about your fundraising activity and where you will donate the money, type up the minutes for that meeting. Give copies of the agenda and minutes for each meeting to your teacher for evaluation.

When each group has finished its meeting(s), report on your group's decision to the class. Discuss how effective your meetings were and any problems your group may have had. Suggest ways in which your meetings could have been improved. Make a list of tips for running and attending successful meetings.

TAKE ACTION ON THE JOB #1

A. Ask your supervisor if you can attend different committee meetings at work as well as your department meeting if you are not already doing so. Take notes during the meeting(s) and compare them to the official minutes when they are distributed.

B. If you work for an incorporated company, find out when the Annual General Meeting is to be held and ask if you can assist in the preparation for it and if you would be able to attend. During the meeting, make notes on the roles of the chairperson, the recording secretary, and the treasurer. Bring the notice of the meeting and the annual report to class for display. Minutes from the previous year's meeting may be available as well.

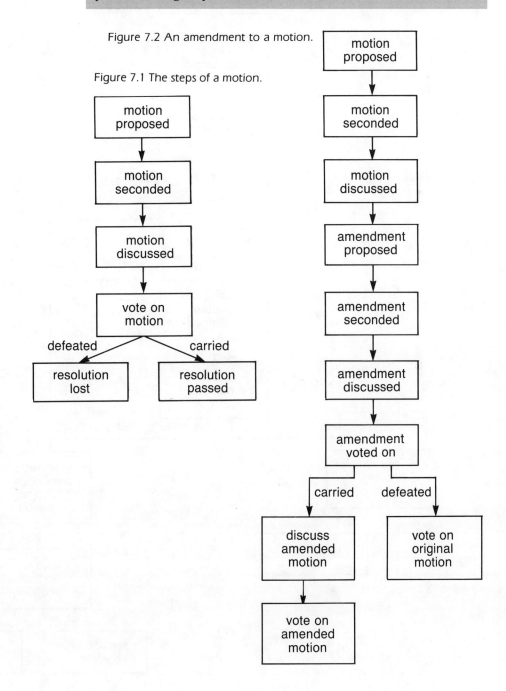

Figure 7.2 An amendment to a motion.

Figure 7.1 The steps of a motion.

Figure 7.3 A motion for closure.

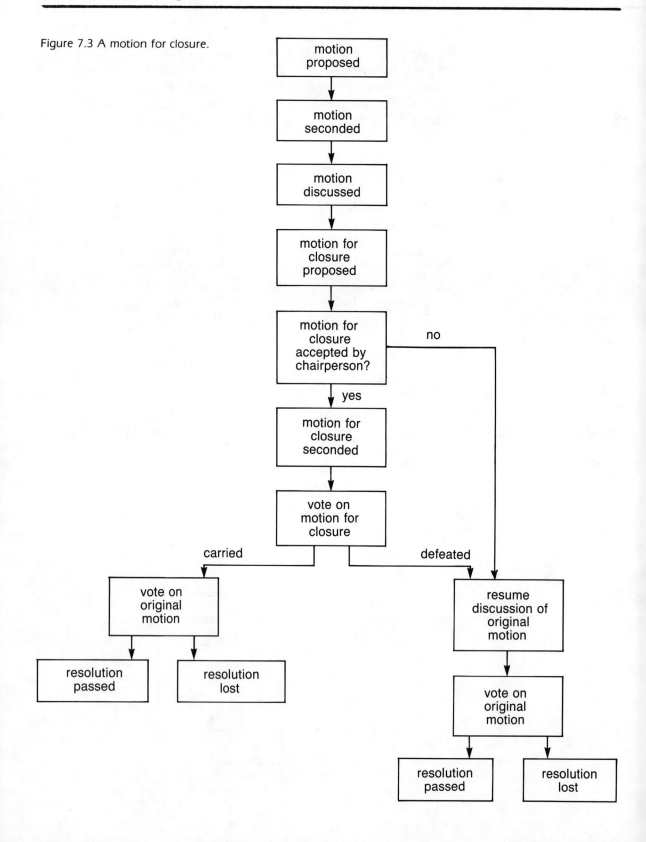

THE BUSINESS OF RESEARCH

8

A problem well stated is a
problem half solved.
CHARLES F. KETTERING

TAKE NOTE
When you have to investigate to find answers to questions or solutions to problems, you are doing research. As a skilled researcher, you will need to know both where to look for answers and how to recognize them when you find them.
A good researcher becomes a human question mark.

Finding information is part of your everyday life. Sometimes you need answers to satisfy your own curiosity; sometimes you need to find information for other people, such as teachers, parents, and employers. In some cases, you will already know the answers yourself. In others you will have to look for information.

TAKE ACTION #1
A. Copy the following sentences in your notebook and find the information you need to complete each one. After each sentence indicate the source of your information.

(i) The producer of my favourite musical album (or tape) is
_____ .

(ii) The year my school was opened is _____ and the name of the school's first principal is _____ .

(iii) My sign of the zodiac (according to the month of my birth) is _____ .

(iv) The sign of the zodiac most romantically suited to mine is _____ .

(v) The number of times I have moved from one residence to another is _____ and the year of each move is _____ .

B. As a class, make a list of all the sources of information you used to answer these questions. Discuss where else you might have looked and who else you might have asked.

In your career you will encounter many situations in which you will be required to find information and solve problems. Sometimes you will have the answer in your head or at your fingertips; sometimes you will not. Then you will have to do research to find it.

Six Steps to Successful Research
1. Identify the problem or question.
2. Identify possible sources of information.
3. Collect the information.
4. Organize the information.
5. Decide how to present the information.
6. Evaluate your work.

Let's work through an example of the use of these steps to solve a specific research problem: how to handle job stress.

Reprinted by permission of United Feature Syndicate, Inc.

Step #1 Identify the Problem or Question
Only after you have answered the following three questions will you know how much research you need to do:

- **What is the problem?** (State it clearly in one or two sentences)
- **What do I already know?** (What information do I already have?)
- **What do I have to find out?** (Make a list of questions which need to be answered.)

Example:
What is the problem?

The question is "How can a person most effectively handle job-related stress?"

What do we already know?

We have some personal experience as employees.

We are aware of some of the commonly held ideas about stress and job-related stress; for example, that some stress is unavoidable and is in fact necessary. However, we aren't sure if any of our ideas are facts or merely assumptions so we will have to confirm that what we think is true during our research.

What do we have to find out?

Here is a list of questions we made to find the information we need to answer the question:

- What is stress? What is job stress?
- What are the symptoms of stress?
- What are the causes of stress?
- What are the most common stressful work situations? Why are they stressful?
- Are some jobs more stressful than others? Which ones? Why?
- How are stress and job productivity related?
- What steps can employers and employees take to help reduce stress levels?
- Can people use stress to their advantage? If so, how?

TAKE ACTION #2

A. Choose one of the following topics for your research project. For Step #1, answer the three questions on p. 201. On your own, decide what the question or problem is and what information is already known. Working with a partner, make a list of questions to be asked. Be specific when listing the information you need to know.

(i) Does working with video display terminals cause health problems?

(ii) Does new technology threaten job security?

(iii) How can employers and employees help to increase job satisfaction and productivity?

(iv) Who should be responsible for pollution control — government or business?

(v) Do unions help or hinder management/employee relations?

(vi) A topic approved by your teacher

STEP #2 *IDENTIFY POSSIBLE SOURCES OF INFORMATION*

Once you have decided what you need to find out, your next step in the research project is to decide where to look for the answer(s). The more you know about your topic, the easier it is to identify possible sources of information.

All sources can be divided into two categories—people who are experts in your area of interest, and materials (written and audio-visual) that contain information about your subject. The following lists will give you some idea of how many resources and sources there are:

Resources—professional and service organizations, businesses, service clubs, public and school libraries, and government departments and agencies.

Sources—encyclopaedias, books, magazines, pamphlets, photographs, films, newspapers, atlases, records, videotapes, computer data bases, and electronic information systems.

Metro weather
Showers tomorrow, high 17C
See page A2

Royal love letters
King wrote of 'months of hell'
See page A3

Rangers oust Caps
Do or die for Leafs tonight
See page B3

FINAL

THE TORONTO STAR

25 CENTS
(35 cents outside central Ontario)
Monday-Friday
paid circulation 518,962

Business

OVERSIZE
001 to 698

The Globe and Mail
Canada's National Newspaper

Institute of Canadian Advertising

CCH
C.C.H. Canadian Limited

Canadian
FINANCIAL
INSTITUTIONS

FRASER
CANADIAN TRADE DIREC.

PRODUCT CLASSIFICATIONS -A to L
VOLUME 1-1985

AIR & GAS COMPRESSORS · PUMPS
POWER TOOLS · AIR HOISTS

INGERSOLL-RAI

VIBRATORY COMPACTORS · ROCK DRILLING EQUIPME
ROAD SURFACE MILLERS · PULP & PAPER PROCESS MACH

Affiliated.

Compressed Air
and Hydraulic
Equipment
for
MINING
CONSTRUCTION
MANUFACTURING

Atlas Copco

Be aware that one source can lead to others. Look at the bibliographies of the books you read for the titles of other books and articles on your topic. Ask the people you talk to if they can recommend any other people or material that might be helpful.

Make a list of all the sources you can think of and add to your list as you continue the project. Check off each source after you use it.

It is a nice gesture (and good business practice) to write thank-you letters to people who have been helpful, especially if they have taken time from their regular jobs to assist you.

Example:
We made this list of places where we could start looking for information about job stress:

• a dictionary (to define stress)
• one Canadian and one American encyclopaedia (to get a general overview of the subject of stress)
• the subject card catalogues in both the school and public libraries (We can look for books, films, and other material under the subject headings "stress" and "job stress." Once we find books on our subject, we can use the table of contents and the index to locate specific information.)
• the Vertical Files in both the school and public libraries (a large filing cabinet that contains newspaper articles and pamphlets on such subjects as "stress" and "employment")
• the *Reader's Guide to Periodical Literature* and the *Business Periodicals Index* (reference guides available in most libraries that list recent magazine articles published on various subjects)
• the ERIC computer data base service available at the Board of Education's professional library (You may be able to find information here with the help of your teacher. Most professional libraries of large organizations and businesses have computer hook-ups to a data base. These bases are valuable sources of information that can be accessed by any employee.)
• our Board of Education film and videotape catalogue (From the booklet we get the titles of two films we can look at on the subject of job stress to see if either would be useful.)
• the local office of Employment and Immigration Canada (the government agency that is responsible for employment related problems. We may be able to get pamphlets here and someone could tell us where we might find other information.)
• a friend is a psychologist who might be able to refer us to a colleague who does research or counselling on job stress (We can also check the phone book's Yellow Pages under "Counselling," "Psychologists," and "Stress Management.")

A school or public library is one of the best places to start looking for research information. The librarian may be able to suggest additional material.

TAKE ACTION #3

A. Working in small groups make a complete list of the sources and resources that you could use to gather information for your research project.

STEP #3 COLLECT THE INFORMATION

Once you have decided where you will look for answers, your next step is collecting and recording the required information. The collecting of information can be divided into two categories:

• collecting information that someone else has previously researched and recorded (secondary information)
• collecting first-hand information that you receive directly from people you interview (primary information)

It is very important that you do some background research (from encyclopaedias, books, magazines, etc.) before you interview anyone. If you research secondary material first, then you will be able to conduct your interviews more efficiently.

When you collect information from secondary sources:

- skim through material first to see if it is a good source of information.
- always record the following information for each source: name of author, publisher, producer; title of source; date and place of publication or production; page number or location of material. You do this so that you can give credit to your sources and so that your research can be verified.
- use point-form notes to record information. When you quote material, make sure it is accurate and put quotation marks around it to identify it. Do not confuse quoting (stating someone's exact words in quotation marks), paraphrasing (stating someone's idea in your own words and giving credit to the source), and plagiarizing (saying someone else's work is your own).
- select only material that deals specifically with your topic. If you find you're gathering too much material, re-read your list of the information you need to know to remind yourself exactly what you want to find out.

When you collect information from primary sources:

• plan your questions before you call or visit the person. Use a steno pad with each question written at the top of a separate page. This allows you to record the person's answers directly below the question asked. Ask the most important questions first, in case you run out of time.

• before you start, ask the person being interviewed if you may quote her or him directly. You will probably be given permission, but if you aren't, you will have to find another person who will give such permission.

• never bring a tape recorder to an interview unless you have been given permission to do so. Use mechanical recording devices only if you and the person being interviewed are comfortable using them.

• record the person's full name (properly spelled) and position in the organization, and the name of the company, agency, or organization for which the person works. You do this so that you can give credit to your sources and so that your research can be verified.

• listen carefully and don't be afraid to ask for clarification if there's something you don't understand.

• if the person whom you have contacted cannot give you the answers you require, always ask if she or he knows anyone who could.

• always send a thank-you note to express your appreciation immediately after the interview.

Use all your organization and communication skills to make interviews as productive and efficient as possible.

Example:

We used index cards to record all our information. On the first card we recorded the definition of stress and the source of the information (the name of the publisher, etc.) for the dictionary we used.

We used several cards to record in point form the general information we gathered from the encyclopaedias. Again, we carefully recorded the source of the information.

Our use of the *Reader's Periodical Guide to Literature* led us to two excellent magazine articles on job stress; one in *Reader's Digest* and the other in *Business Week*. We also made notes from one pamphlet found in our school library's Vertical File and from a film we found at the public library.

A book by a Canadian, Dr. Hans Selye, called *Stress Without Distress*, proved helpful and the bibliography provided us with more leads.

We phoned an industrial psychologist and arranged an interview. The psychologist gave us tips on how to reduce job stress and gave us copies of several articles to read.

Dictionary

- Oxford Dictionary of Current English
  ed. R.E. Allen, Oxford University Press, 1985, England
- stress "pressure or tension"; "demand on physical or mental energy, distress caused by this"

Stress Without Distress #4   Selye, Hans

p. 84 - work is a necessity
       - keeps our minds active, this is more important than status and financial security

> Interview – Ms. Jane Orton   555-0101
> Industrial Psychologist
>
> Q. How can an employee lower the stress level at work?
>
> A. "Taking a break from the actual job site works best – take a walk or do some exercises."

TAKE ACTION #4

A. Refer to your list of sources and resources and make arrangements for interviews and collecting information. Carefully record the information you need and keep your notes. They will be evaluated for accuracy, completeness, and usefulness.

STEP #4 ORGANIZE THE INFORMATION

After you have collected information from various sources, you must organize what you have found. How you organize your information will depend on the information itself and on the purpose of your research. The list of organizers in chapter 2 (p. 40) may help you decide.

Example

When we looked at the information we collected, we realized that we could divide it into two sections—background information on the causes and symptoms of stress and how to deal with stress effectively.

For the first section we used the cause and effect organizer to explain job stress. For the second we decided to use the general to specific organizer to describe how to deal with stress. For example, we might suggest using exercise to help fight the effects of stress and then give specific exercises to do.

TAKE ACTION #5
A. Decide which organizer will help you present your information most clearly and effectively. Organize the information you have collected.

STEP #5   DECIDE HOW TO PRESENT THE INFORMATION
Up to now in the research process, you have been mainly a receiver of messages. You have sent a few messages asking for information but you have spent most of your time finding and collecting material to help you solve your problem. At this point you must decide which medium you are going to use to present your information or solution. You have several choices—an oral presentation, an audio-visual recording, a written reply (such as memo, letter, report form, chart, or graph), or some combination of these.

In choosing the most effective medium for the delivery of your information you must consider:

• audience (Is the audience already familiar with the subject? What level of language should you use? Knowing as much as possible about your audience will help you decide on the format you should use.)

• purpose (Are you explaining something to someone or are you trying to persuade someone to do something? Do you need to phone an answer to someone immediately, or is a careful analysis required? Understanding the purpose of your research will help you decide on the best medium and format.)
• content (Is the information complicated or easy to grasp? Would charts, graphs, or pictures help your audience understand the subject better?)

A written report might be necessary if the information is complex and will need to be re-read. An oral presentation might be better in a situation where there may be questions. Consider the features of each medium before you decide.

Example
We decided on a combination of media to answer the question:

"How can a person most effectively handle job-related stress?"

First we considered our audience—our colleagues at work. We did not choose a formal report because the language levels are, for the most part, informal. The familiarity with the topic varied from person to person. We assumed most people were aware of the subject but had little actual knowledge of it.

The purpose of our research is to describe and explain job-related stress. We wanted to show our audience how to recognize and deal with it.

The material itself was straightforward. We decided to give a short oral presentation so that people could ask questions. We made brief notes to define stress and job stress. We also explained the causes and symptoms.

We made some graphs to help explain the relationship between productivity and job stress and charts to show the most stressful job and work situations. We explained why it is impossible, even undesirable, to avoid stress completely.

We decided to give out a written list of tips to help people reduce stress or use it to their advantage. People will be able to refer to this list later, if they need it.

TAKE ACTION #6

A. Decide what is the most effective way to present your information. Write down your decision and your reasons for it.

STEP #6   EVALUATE YOUR WORK

The last step in the business of research is evaluating your own work. Ask yourself the following questions:

- Did I gather my information from the best sources? Is it correct? Is it current?
- Have I answered the question and/or solved the problem?
- Is the information factual and complete? Is my presentation of it clear?

Example

We used the dictionary and encyclopaedias to give us a general overview of the subject. Then we used recent sources—magazine articles, pamphlets, and a film—to round out our knowledge of current information. We checked our assumptions to make sure they were correct. Talking to an expert in the field helped confirm that the ideas we collected were sound and up to date.

We answered the list of questions with which we started (p. 201). According to our sources we explained the most common causes of stress and described the symptoms. We also presented effective strategies for dealing with stress on the job. We considered the best means of presenting our information (according to audience, purpose, and content) and think we have chosen the most appropriate media.

TAKE ACTION #7

A. Refer to the research project checklist on p. 212 to help you prepare a brief, point-form evaluation of the research you did. List any difficulties you may have had and suggest how they might be avoided in the future.

RESEARCH PROJECT CHECKLIST

When you do research, you should:

- ☐ identify the question or problem and what you have to find out.
- ☐ gather information from the most appropriate sources.
- ☐ consult a wide range of sources to make sure the information you get is correct, current, and complete.
- ☐ organize your information according to the content and purpose.
- ☐ present your information in the most appropriate format to make it easy to understand.
- ☐ make sure your information solves the original problem or answers the original question.

B. Give your teacher your research material and your evaluation of it. After your teacher has evaluated your work, put all your research material into your writing folder to be used in another activity later.

THE BUSINESS OF REPORT WRITING

9

Reports are the means by which business substitutes knowledge for guesswork.
VANESSA DEAN ARNOLD

MEMO

To: Students in Business English
From: Judi Misener and Sandra Steele
Re: Report Writing

Our editors asked us to include a chapter on report writing. We did some research and found out that report writing in business and industry is very different from the kind of report writing you normally do in school (e.g., ''The Causes of World War I'' in history class or ''Why Dodos are Extinct'' for a science course.)

There are two types of reports you may be asked to write as an employee. The most common is the **informal** or **short report** — e.g., an accident report, a progress report, or a proposal report. This type of report is examined in the first part of this chapter. In fact, the material is presented in the format of an informal report.

Occasionally you may be asked to write a **formal** or **long report**. This type of report is examined in the second part of the chapter and is presented in the format of a formal report.

Read the chapter carefully. Follow our examples and Take Action.

Good Luck!

JM
SS.

INFORMAL REPORTS

MEMO

TO: Students in Business English
FROM: Judi Misener and Sandra Steele
RE: Writing Informal Reports in Business and Industry

RECOMMENDATIONS
When you are asked to write a report you are being asked to investigate, assemble, and organize facts in order to describe a situation or solve a problem.
   We recommend that you first of all consider:
(1) the report's purpose — why the presentation has to be made
(2) the report's audience — who will receive the report
(3) the appropriate format you should use when you present your report

MAJOR CONSIDERATIONS IN INFORMAL REPORT WRITING
Purpose
As a member of a working team in a business or industry, you may be asked to assemble and present information so that an important decision can be made. It is crucial that you understand exactly why you have been asked to collect and present information. Usually someone you work with or for will tell you directly; for example, ''We need more information about the two different types of computer systems that the boss must decide between for the office. Find out comparative costs, capabilities, and expansion potential.'' If instructions like that don't make sense to you, then ask for clarification. This way, no time will be wasted researching and writing unnecessary information. Knowing the precise purpose of an assigned report will save you and your company valuable time and effort.

The Audience
The audience of your report is the receiver of your message. You must find out how knowledgeable your audience is about the subject of your report. Take time to discuss with the person assigning the report exactly how much information is required. Identify what the receiver already knows and what you are expected to fill in. Once you have established the scope of the assignment, you should apply the six steps to successful research (see p. 200) to solving the problem.

The Format
An informal or short report is presented in memo format. If the report is sent to someone outside your company, a covering letter is always attached explaining why the report is being sent. These reports rarely exceed three to five pages in length.

The report is usually organized into three parts:

- recommendations
- body (major considerations)
- conclusion

Sometimes if the receiver of your report is rushed for time, only the recommendations will be read. That is why you present them first. If the receiver has more time or needs more information, your detailed major considerations will be studied. Headings help the receiver grasp the most important ideas you are presenting. Your headings organize the material so that the information can be understood easily.

CONCLUSION
Informal report writing is a common method of business communication. It involves the collection and presentation of information that is required in the decision-making process. It is your task as a report writer to be accurate and concise in your research and delivery. Understanding the report's purpose and knowing your receiver will help you assemble the kind of information that will be most useful in solving the problem at hand. Using a well-organized format will ensure that the information will be clearly understood.

TAKE ACTION #1

A. Choose two of the following situations and for each one write an outline arranging the necessary information in logical order and the rough draft of an informal report. Keep in mind the purpose, audience, and format as you proceed.

(i) Before writing a letter of recommendation for you, your homeroom teacher asks you to prepare a progress report on your performance during the school year.

(ii) Prepare an accident report about any situation that you know of involving personal injury. The person injured could be a friend, a relative, a fellow employee, or school acquaintance. Your report should include recommendations to prevent others from suffering similar injury. The audience of your report could be your school principal, the owner of the business where the injured person works, or the Workers' Compensation Board (or similar provincial agency responsible for worker safety).

(iii) The supervisor at your part-time job wants you to write a report on the most important task or procedure that you perform. The report will be used as a form of instruction for other people performing this task at new branch plants or offices. If appropriate, include suggestions or recommendations for improving your working conditions to perform the task better.

(iv) You would like to see an important change made in a particular procedure used either in one of your classes or at your job. You have decided the best way to get attention concerning this matter is to write a report proposing the change.

(v) You have just returned from a meeting, conference, or business trip and you have been asked by the organization that sent you to write a short report describing your impressions. You have also been asked to give your opinion about the usefulness of sending someone the next time this meeting or conference is held.

B. Working with a writing partner, exchange the rough drafts of your reports and carefully edit each other's material. Attach a list of suggestions your partner might use to improve each report.

C. Submit the final draft of one of your reports to your teacher for evaluation. Refer to the checklist on p. 220 to help you write a brief, point-form evaluation of the other report. A time will be set aside for you and your teacher to discuss your individual evaluations.

A COMPARISON

THE INFORMAL REPORT	THE FORMAL REPORT

PURPOSE

All reports have the general purpose of investigating, assembling, and organizing the facts in order to describe a situation or to solve a problem. It is your job as the report writer to be very clear about the purpose of every report before you start to write.

AUDIENCE

The informal report is usually written for an audience the report writer knows.

For this reason the language level is usually informal.

The formal report is usually written for an audience with which the writer is not necessarily familiar. Therefore, your language level is more formal than it is in an informal report.

LENGTH

The informal report can be a single page, but it is never much longer than five pages.

The formal report is seldom less than eight to ten pages and can be hundreds of pages in length.

FORMAT

The informal report is usually written as a memo, broken into these three parts:
(1) recommendations
(2) body (major considerations)
(3) conclusion

The formal report follows the standard format expected in the business community which consists of these eight parts:
(1) the title page
(2) the letter of transmittal
(3) the table of contents
(4) the preface
(5) the summary
(6) the body — purpose, method, findings, conclusions
(7) recommendations
(8) the bibliography

RESEARCH

The informal report is often based on information the sender has gained from personal experience (e.g., the accident or the excursion report). Some additional information gathering may be required for the proposal report (e.g., making telephone calls, interviewing a few people, or reading information provided by two different manufacturers of office or shop equipment). This kind of research can be done in a few hours.

The formal report is always based on information gathered through extensive research. The research methods used most often are:
- personal interviews based on formal questionnaires
- background research done in a public or company library
- collecting data from the company's own files (e.g., sales figures)

The time allotted to research by a single individual writing a formal report can range from several days to several months.

INFORMAL REPORT WRITING CHECKLIST

When you write an informal report, you should:

☐ make sure you completely understand the exact purpose of the report.
☐ find out exactly how much the person assigning the report and the audience already know about the topic, and what kind of new information you are expected to uncover and present.
☐ know enough about your audience in order to use the appropriate language level in your report.
☐ break up the presentation of your material into the following parts—recommendations, major considerations, and conclusion.
☐ use the recommendations section to give your opinions or make suggestions.
☐ use the major considerations section to present the support data for your recommendations.
☐ use headings to mark off the various aspects of your topic clearly.
☐ use the conclusions section of the report to summarize your findings.
☐ proofread your report to make sure that all ideas are clear, concise, courteous, and correct.
☐ proofread for spelling, grammar, and typing errors.

FORMAL REPORTS

The rest of this chapter is set up as a formal report using:

(1) title page
(2) letter of transmittal
(3) table of contents
(4) preface
(5) summary
(6) body of the report, including the purpose, the method, the findings, and the conclusion
(7) recommendations
(8) bibliography

The formal report is used in business to communicate the results of an investigation of some major problem or situation and is written to describe:

- the specific methods used to collect the data
- the data or information that was found
- the investigator's recommendation(s) for solving the problem

FORMAL REPORT WRITING

Judi Misener
Sandra Steele

Prepared for:
The Students in Business English
March 31, 19—

(THE TITLE PAGE)

March 31, 19___

Students in Business English
Hometown High School
456 Mark Street
Quebec City, Quebec
G1P 2Q7

Dear Students:

   We take pleasure in submitting to you our report on the subject of
formal report writing. This is the letter of transmittal. Such a letter
is only written and included as part of a formal report when you
send your report to someone outside your company. The letter
serves as an introduction to your report and can include:

   • an announcement that the report is now being submitted to
the person who requested it
   • a reference to some prominent feature of the report
   • a suggestion that further investigation may be needed to
solve the problem

   The final sentence of your letter simply thanks the receiver of the
report for showing interest in your work.

                    Yours sincerely,

                    Judi Misener
                    Sandra Steele

                    Judi Misener
                    Sandra Steele

:mh

TABLE OF CONTENTS

PREFACE

The preface is the introduction to your report. It has three purposes.

(1) *It explains why your report was written.* Were you asked to write it by some individual or group? Or did you undertake to write it on your own in order to convince an individual or group of your point of view?

For example: We decided to write this report because we want you to be prepared to write formal reports when you go out to work.

(2) *It refers briefly to the content of the report* (especially if there are any features that are unusual).

For example: Every part of this report is illustrated by an excerpt or sample from an actual report entitled *Youth Unemployment in Metropolitan Toronto*, prepared by Laura C. Johnson and Jeffrey G. Reitz (Toronto: Social Planning Council of Metropolitan Toronto, 1981).

(3) *It outlines the type of research you did in preparing the report.*

For example: In our research for this report we looked at several formal business reports and we read a selection of books and papers on the subject of formal report writing.

SUMMARY

> The objective of this study has been to describe the nature and extent of employment and unemployment among youth, and to examine some of its causes and consequences. Particular attention is paid to the attitude of young adults toward work and the way in which these attitudes might affect their labour force participation.

The summary of a formal report is a short statement which highlights the main ideas covered in the body of the report, as well as a brief explanation of the major conclusions or recommendations of the report. The summary answers the question "What is this report about?" You include the summary at the beginning of a report so that anyone who requires a quick overview of your report can find it there.

This study provides little support for the notion that youth unemployment can be attributed to poor work attitudes, a decline in the work ethic, or excessive expectations on the part of youth. Rather, current levels of youth unemployment reflect a pattern that can be expected when jobs are in short supply. The youngest, least educated, and least well-connected youth are most vulnerable to unemployment. Some young workers have high expectations, but this does not prevent them from working. However, it can lead them from job to job which antagonizes some employers.

BODY OF THE REPORT
Purpose

The purpose of this report is to present the results of an investigation into the causes of youth unemployment.

In the purpose of the formal report you outline very briefly why you have written your report. You answer the question "What is the problem?"

Official unemployment rates among the young are higher than for older workers. We wanted to find out why this is so.

Method
In the method portion of your report, you state how you collected the information you have included in the report. You answer the question "What sources of information were used?"

Survey field work was conducted between May and August of this year.

Findings

Youth unemployment is not the result of lack of motivation on the part of young people. Although the percentage of youth (ages 16 to 24) who are unemployed is much higher than the unemployment rate among older workers (Figure 1), the percentage of unemployed youth has not risen any more rapidly than the percentage for older workers. This indicates that external factors (e.g., lack of demand for all workers in the market place) have caused a general rise in unemployment.

The findings section of your report includes the data that you have collected and organized. The information that you present here (including charts, graphs, tables, etc.) supports the recommendations that you will make later.

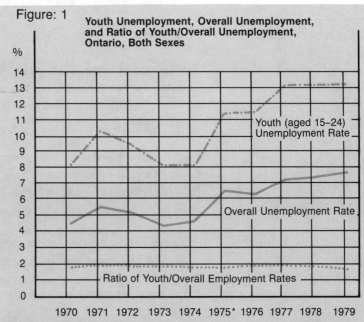

Figure: 1

Youth Unemployment, Overall Unemployment, and Ratio of Youth/Overall Unemployment, Ontario, Both Sexes

Source: Statistics Canada
*Note: Data for 1975–1979 are based on the revised Labour Force Survey definition of Unemployment (Thériault, 1977)

Table 19 shows the opinions of the employers we interviewed regarding the causes of youth unemployment.

Table 19
Employer Views on Causes of Youth Unemployment

Reason	Number of Employers
Poor economy and job shortages	11
Problems with the educational system	5
Inappropriate work attitudes among youth	5
Availability of social benefits (UIC and welfare)	4
Lack of job search and employment skills	2

> Most employers felt that many existing government programs directed at reducing youth unemployment were ineffective. The best ones, according to the majority of employers, had a training component. Gaining some form of practical, technical training was considered essential in a highly competitive job market.

Conclusion

> This study provides little support for the idea that youth unemployment can be attributed to poor work attitudes, a decline in the work ethic, or excessive expectations and a "spoiled brat" syndrome.

The conclusion portion of your report is optional. If you have presented your conclusions in the summary of the report and you feel that there is no need to repeat them, you can eliminate this part.

> Rather, youth unemployment appears to follow a pattern expected in a period where jobs in general are in short supply.

RECOMMENDATIONS

> Since the data show that unemployed youth already have lowered their expectations, measures such as reducing unemployment insurance would be a cruel and ineffective step to take.
> Youth job-retraining, as a preparation for gaining employment where there is a demand, is effective, as long as young workers are not shifted to dead-end jobs.

This is the most important portion of your report. It is the sum total of everything else you have included. Your recommendations are your solutions to the problem you have investigated.

> Job creation and government measures intended to stimulate the general economy will deal most effectively with youth unemployment.

BIBLIOGRAPHY

Arnold, Vanessa. "The Business Report: A Basic Element in Basic Business Education". *Journal of Business Education*, 58, No. 4, January 1983.

Bell, James B., and Edward P. J. Corbett. *The Little English Handbook for Canadians*. Toronto: John Wiley & Sons Canada Ltd., 1982.

Coggins, Gordon. *A Guide to Writing Essays and Research Papers*. Toronto: Van Nostrand Reinhold Ltd., 1977.

Easton, Thomas A. *How to Write a Readable Business Report*. Homewood, Illinois: Dow Jones–Irwin, 1983.

Farmiloe, Dorothy. *Communication for Business Students*. Toronto: Holt, Rinehart and Winston of Canada Ltd., 1981.

Johnson, Laura C., and Jeffrey G. Reitz. *Youth Unemployment in Metropolitan Toronto*. Toronto: Social Planning Council of Metropolitan Toronto, 1981.

When you have finished preparing the body of your report, you must give credit in a bibliography to all the sources of information you have used. This includes books, magazine articles, government documents, films, radio and television broadcasts, records, lectures, and personal interviews. The bibliography makes it possible for the receiver of your report to double-check your facts or to find further information from the same sources.

The bibliography is organized in alphabetical order by authors' last names (or by titles if the author is unknown). The first line of each entry begins at the left-hand margin with the following lines indented.

The three main divisions of author, title, and publishing data are separated by periods.

The publication data follow this order: place of publication, name of the publisher, and publication date.

FURTHER EXAMPLES

Encyclopaedia article, signed:
Cameron, A.G.W. "Solar System," *The World Book Enclycopaedia*,
    1972 ed., 18:474. Chicago: Field Enterprises.
Encyclopaedia article, unsigned:
"Icebreaker," *Encyclopaedia Americana*, 1971 ed., 14:707.
Government publication:
Government of Canada, Department of National Revenue. *Tax
    Reform and You—Valuation Day.* Undated pamphlet.
Letter or memo:
Goodale, D. J. Letter to G. Loggins, Aug. 18, 1985.
Record or tape:
U2. *War*. Island Records Ltd. ISL-67.
Film:
Fueter, Heinrich. *Waste—the Penalty of Affluence.* Condor Films,
    on behalf of World Wildlife Fund,
    Colour, 18 mins., 1968.
Radio or television broadcast:
Levine, Otto. Interviewed by Margo Lane on "Money Matters."
    CBC Television, June 17, 1985.
Personal Interview:
Logan, Andrew, Head of History, Abbot High School. "The
    Influence of the Depression on Employment Rates." An inter-
    view, May 3, 1984.

FORMAL REPORT WRITING CHECKLIST

When you write a formal report, you should:

☐ make sure you completely understand the exact purpose of the report.

☐ find out exactly how much the person assigning the report and the audience already know about the topic and what kind of new information you are expected to uncover and present.

☐ realize that you do not know everyone in your audience who will read your report; therefore you should write the report in formal language.

☐ write a letter of transmittal if your report is going to someone outside your company.

☐ use the preface section of your report to alert your audience to anything unusual in the body of your report.

☐ use the summary to inform your audience right away about the major conclusions of your report.

☐ organize the information you have collected into these sections of the body of your report—purpose, method, findings, and conclusions.

☐ prepare a thorough, standardized bibliography for your report, listing every source of information used.

☐ proofread your report to make sure that all ideas are clear, concise, courteous, and correct.

☐ proofread for spelling, grammar, and typing errors.

TAKE ACTION #2

A. Take the information you gathered for chapter 8, "The Business of Research," from your writing folder. Depending on how you decided to present your material in TAKE ACTION #6 (p. 211), use your research information to prepare either an informal report (4–5 pages long) or an oral presentation (10–20 minutes long). Your teacher will outline a schedule for completion which will include a personal interview to discuss your own progress and a class discussion of any problems or suggestions.

If you are doing a written report, refer to the checklist on p. 231 of this chapter for help in preparing it. If you are making an oral presentation, refer to the checklist in chapter 6, "The Business of Speaking," (p. 161) to help you prepare it. Write point-form notes of the material you will be using and give these notes to your teacher for evaluation after your presentation.

JOB SEARCH IV

Getting Hired

All your hard work has paid off and you have been granted an interview. Congratulations! You probably feel excited and nervous. The confidence you have gained from developing your ability to communicate effectively can help you overcome your nervousness, but there are also other steps you can take to prepare yourself for an interview.

BEFORE YOUR INTERVIEW

Before you go for an interview, you should find out as much as possible about the company; for example, how large it is (number of employees and offices) and the products and services it offers. This information will help you answer questions during your job interview as well as help you decide if the company and the job are right for you.

If you have a personal contact at that business, that's a good place to start asking questions. If not, information on most companies is available at the public library (in professional and trade directories), or you can phone the company and ask to have any material such as promotional brochures, employee newsletters, or annual reports sent to you.

GETTING DOWN TO BUSINESS #1

A. Choose one of the companies you identified in your list of leads from Job Search II (p. 58). Using the techniques you learned in "The Business of Research," collect as much information about the company as you can. Write down the information in brief point-form notes for your teacher to evaluate.

It is a good idea to be prepared to answer any questions you may be asked in an interview. No matter what you are asked, you should be able to give a positive and well-thought-out answer. For example, if you are asked about your work experience, don't be afraid to admit it if you don't have any experience in that type of job. But don't stop there — tell the interviewer about any skills you have that would be valuable for that position or emphasize your interest in that field and eagerness to learn new skills.

Here are some of the most frequently asked questions and some hints on how to answer them:

Why do you want to work here?
Outline your interest in that career, in the company's products or services, and the opportunity to learn new skills, etc. Your answer will demonstrate that you have researched the company prior to the interview and that you are seriously interested in working there.

Tell me about yourself.
You must be careful to appear confident but not conceited when you answer this question. Prepare your answer very carefully. Outline your interests, skills, and achievements in three to five sentences.

Have you had any experience in this type of work?
If you have, explain what it is. If you don't have any, be positive by outlining the skills, courses, and experiences you have had that would be valuable for this type of job.

What qualifications or special skills do you bring to this job?
Refer to your résumé if you need to. Be thorough and confident about what you can do. Accentuate the positive.

How did you get along with your previous employer?
Stress that you had a good working relationship if that was the case. Be honest if there was a conflict but do not go into detail or put all the blame on the other person. Indicate you have learned from your past experiences.

What did you like most or least about your previous job (or school)?
Try to relate what you liked most to the particular job or career. Be honest about what you didn't like but try to minimize its importance. Every job has its area of difficulty but criticizing the other company or your school will not make you look good.

What activities are you involved with in your spare time?
Your answer gives the interviewer insight into your abilities and attitude. Activities that are not related to your job indicate to employers that you have well-rounded interests and show initiative and enthusiasm.

What are your long-term career plans?
Show ambition but be realistic — talk in general terms. For example, mention a supervisor's position if that is what you wish but do not be so exacting that you mention the company and the salary as well. You must show that you can be flexible and realistic.

Are you willing to relocate?
Be honest — only you know the answer to this one.

When can you start work?
Knowing this demonstrates you have prepared yourself for the interview and seriously contemplated working.

Why should I hire you?
This question is a challenge — do not be intimidated by it. Be positive and matter-of-fact. A sample answer is: "I believe I am well qualified for the position and have the attitude and interest to be successful and that I will contribute positively to your company."

GETTING DOWN TO BUSINESS #2
A. Working in partners, go through each of the previous questions and compose sample answers. Discuss how effective each answer is and suggest any improvements that could be made.

B. Study your education and work backgrounds objectively and list any weaknesses (e.g., lack of work experience, being fired from a job) you think an interviewer may ask about. For each problem, prepare a possible answer that stresses the positive aspects or shows what you have learned from the situation.

Asking questions during the interview shows planning and initiative. You may want clarification of some of the points mentioned during the interview or you may want to learn more about the job and working conditions. Unless you are offered the job during the interview, it is not usually a good idea to ask about salary, vacation, and benefits. Here is a list of possible questions you could prepare:

- What are the company's greatest strengths?
- What is the turnover of employees?
- What do you see in the future for this company?
- What characteristics do you look for in your employees?
- What kind of on-the-job training is available?
- Could you elaborate on the duties and responsibilities of the position?
- When will you be making your decision about this position?

THE INTERVIEW

The most important asset you can bring to your interviews is a confident and positive attitude. This is your chance to use your communication skills (both verbal and non-verbal) to show the interviewer that you are the best person for the job. Here are some points to remember:

Make a good first impression
- Dress appropriately — be neat and businesslike.
- Arrive at the company a few minutes early so that you will be on time for the interview.
- Greet the interviewer by name.
- Be pleasant and courteous but not over-friendly.

During the interview
- Listen carefully to each question. Let the interviewer finish before you start to answer.
- Speak clearly and slowly. Answer the interviewer's questions completely and ask any questions you have, but don't talk just to cover up your nervousness.
- Be honest — a lie detected later could cost you your job.
- Have ready any information the interviewer may request (e.g., a list of references, extra copies of your résumé).
- Show interest non-verbally as well as verbally through the use of posture and eye contact. Avoid such negative non-verbal communication as chewing gum, smoking, or fidgeting.
- Make sure you understand what is expected of you in any pre-employment tests you are asked to take. (These are tests for such things as spelling, typing, and mathematics.) Don't get flustered — just do the test as well as you can.

Closing the interview
- Watch for non-verbal signs from the interviewer that the interview is coming to a close — shuffling papers, moving in the chair. If the interview has not covered all the points you feel it should, take the initiative and briefly outline them.
- Thank the interviewer.

Interviewers often complete an interview appraisal sheet to help them remember each interview when they are making their final decision. Read the sample on p. 244 to see the type of qualities people look for during an interview.

GETTING DOWN TO BUSINESS #3

A. Working in small groups, take turns role-playing job interviews. One person will do the interviewing, one will be the job applicant, and the others will evaluate the interview using a copy of the interview checklist on p. 245. Draw up a schedule to make sure each person in the group has a turn being interviewed and conducting an interview.

As the applicant: prepare for your interview by following the suggestions outlined previously. Give your interviewer copies of your résumé and the information you gathered on a company in Getting Down to Business #1 (p. 234).

As the interviewer: Using the material you have been given, prepare questions to ask the job applicant. (Remember that under the Canadian Charter of Rights, it is illegal to discriminate on the basis of age, sex, mental or physical handicap or disability, race, religion, national or ethnic origin, or colour. Compose your questions carefully.) After the interview, fill out a copy of the interview appraisal checklist (p. 244).

After each interview discuss how effective it was, referring to the interview evaluation checklists. Discuss how each applicant might improve job interview skills. As you continue to role-play the job interviews, keep a list of any tips or suggestions your group comes up with to share with the class later.

INTERVIEW FOLLOW-UP

Following-up after an interview is an important part of your job search. Going that extra step demonstrates to an employer that you are organized, enthusiastic, and thorough. It may be the one factor that distinguishes you from other equally qualified applicants. And even if you don't get this job, your follow-up may impress the employer enough to remember you when the next job becomes available.

You can contact the individual who interviewed you by:

- making a return visit two or three days after your interview.
- telephoning two or three days after your interview.
- writing a thank-you letter mailed immediately after your interview.

Whether you visit, phone, or write, here are the key points you should make:

- Identify or reintroduce yourself.
  "Hello, my name is Amity Popovski. I had an interview with you last Wednesday for the position of layout artist."
- Add any additional points you might not have covered in the interview.
  "I did not mention that I was the editor of the school yearbook which involved a great deal of layout experience."
- Emphasize that you are still interested in the job.
  "Mrs. Keyes, I was impressed with your business. I am still very interested in working with you."
- Find out if a hiring decision has been made.
  "Have you reached a decision?" If a decision has been made and you did not get the job, ask the interviewer how you might have created a better impression. Information about how you might improve is valuable for future interviews. Make this a learning experience.
- Thank the interviewer for seeing you or for talking with you.

GETTING DOWN TO BUSINESS #4
A. Working in the same groups as for Getting Down to Business #3 (p. 239), practise making follow-up calls for the job interviews you had. As before, after each call discuss how effective the conversation was and suggest any improvements the job applicant might make.

B. Write a follow-up letter for the job interview you had. Refer to the following sample as a guide.

95 Quinland Road,
St. Catharines, Ontario
L2S 1Y6

January 30, 19__

Ms. Fran Miller
Success Business Centre
900 Park Avenue
Niagara Falls, Ontario
L2G 2X2

Dear Ms. Miller:

Thank you for interviewing me for the job as sales manager with your company. I feel that my past sales experience would be an asset in this challenging position.

I thought you would be interested to know that after our interview, I was selected by the provincial government to sit on a special panel to review proposals for their advertising campaigns. I think this will give me invaluable experience in my career.

Thank you again for the interview. I will phone you in a few days to find out your decision.

Yours sincerely,

Les Mitchell

Les Mitchell

These are the most common reasons people aren't hired, according to a study done at Northwestern University.

1. Poor personal appearance
2. Arrogant, conceited attitude
3. Unable to communicate clearly—poor voice, diction, grammar
4. No clear plans for career
5. Low enthusiasm and interest
6. Lack of confidence and poise
7. Little participation in activities
8. Over-emphasis on money
9. Poor school record
10. Too demanding — wants to start at the top
11. Evasive, makes excuses
12. Lack of sensitivity, tact
13. Lack of maturity
14. Lack of courtesy
15. Criticizes previous employers
16. Lack of etiquette, manners
17. Dislike of school
18. Seems listless, not energetic
19. Poor eye contact
20. Poor handshake

There are other situations after an interview that may also require letters:

- to accept an offer of employment
- acknowledging a rejection by thanking the company for considering you (This could be of benefit if another opportunity with the same company opens later.)
- declining an offer
- explaining that you are no longer available (If you accept a job offer with another company you should inform any company to whom you have applied for a position that you are no longer available.)

EVALUATING A JOB OFFER

After all the hard work you do to find a job, your immediate reaction to any job offer is usually to take it. But even if jobs are not plentiful, it's best to think carefully before you accept a job—if you're unhappy, it just means you'll have to start looking all over again.

Your teacher will give you a copy of the checklist on p. 246 for your Job Search Kit. It contains some questions you should ask yourself when considering a job offer. But remember that not every job has to be perfect—for example, when you are first starting your career, you may accept a lower salary just to get some experience in your field.

INTERVIEW APPRAISAL
Name: Interviewed By:
Address: Date:
Phone:

A = Excellent   B = Good   C = Unacceptable

Item	A	B	C	Comments
Arrival — on time or late with no reason given?				
Résumé/Application Form — neat and complete or messy and incomplete?				
Appearance — well-groomed or careless about appearance?				
Voice and Vocabulary — expressive with effective vocabulary or dull with poor word usage?				
Participation in Conversation — answered fully and asked questions or too talkative; too reserved; evasive?				
Attitude — energetic and enthusiastic or bored, flippant?				
Poise — self-confident, arrogant, or too nervous?				
Manner — courteous and pleasant, over-friendly, or too shy?				
Interest in Job — did company research or no knowledge of company?				
Career Plans — has clear goals and ambitions or indecisive, not ambitious?				
Work Experience — has skills needed or not? Is willing to be trained?				

INTERVIEW CHECKLIST

Date:

Company: Interviewer:

	Yes	No
Were you on time for the interview?	☐	☐
Were you dressed appropriately?	☐	☐
Were you friendly and courteous?	☐	☐
Were you relaxed?	☐	☐
Did the conversation flow smoothly?	☐	☐
Did you know enough about the company?	☐	☐
Did you answer all questions honestly, directly, and thoroughly?	☐	☐

These questions were new to you:

_____

_____

Practise answers to these questions:

_____

_____

Your impression of the interviewer:

_____

_____

Your impression of the job:

_____

_____

Your impression of the company:

_____

_____

Date the decision will be made:

Date of follow-up call or letter:

General Comments:

_____

_____

_____

JOB EVALUATION CHECKLIST

- ☐ Do I clearly understand the responsibilities of the job? Is it what I want to do? Does it suit my personality?
- ☐ Even if it isn't the perfect job for me, will it help further my career or will it restrict my job search in the future?
- ☐ Will I learn new skills? If I need more training, will the company pay for it?
- ☐ Are the hours acceptable? Will I have to work overtime?
- ☐ Is the salary enough? Are there other benefits (e.g., medical)?
- ☐ Is the location convenient?
- ☐ Will I have to travel?
- ☐ Is the job environment acceptable (e.g., cleanliness, adequate ventilation)?
- ☐ Is there job security?
- ☐ Will I be required to join a union?
- ☐ Is there a high staff turnover? If so, why?
- ☐ Is there a chance for advancement with the company? Do they promote from within the firm?

BACK
TO
BASICS

FOR YOUR INFORMATION

GRAMMAR

Grammar is a set of language guidelines that govern how we put words together correctly in sentences. The proper use of grammar makes your messages clear. Improper usage leads to confusion.

There are eight different kinds of words in English grammar: nouns, pronouns, verbs, adjectives, adverbs, prepositions, conjunctions, and articles.

Finally,	she	gave	the	customer	several
(adverb)	(pronoun)	(verb)	(article)	(noun)	(adjective)

papers	and	pictures	from	the	file.
(noun)	(conjunction)	(noun)	(preposition)	(article)	(noun)

NOUNS

A noun is the name of a person, place, or thing. Nouns may be classified in different ways.

Common nouns name general persons, places, or things.
— boy, city, doll
Proper nouns name some specific persons, places, or things.
— Frank, Regina, City Hall
Collective nouns stand for many of one thing.
— *crowd* of people, *herd* of cattle, *gaggle* of geese
Abstract nouns name ideas rather than things.
— love, freedom, evil
Concrete nouns name things you can perceive through your senses.
— log, house, dog

Nouns can be singular (boy, apple, fear) or plural (boys, apples, fears).

Nouns can be used in sentences in the following ways:

• as the subject of the sentence.
— *Mary* is going.

• as the predicate nominative (the word that completes the meaning or description of the subject).
— She is a *teacher*.

• as the object of the verb.
— The bookkeeper mailed the *statements*.

• as the object of a preposition.
— Send a copy of the *letter* today.

PRONOUNS

A pronoun is used in place of a noun.

— Mary is tired. *She* wants to go home.
— *He* is finished with *those.*
— To *whom* should *I* give these books?

There are many different types of pronouns:

	Subjective Form (performing actions)	Objective Form (receiving actions)
Personal	I	me
	we	us
	you	you
	he	him
	she	her
	they	them
Relative	who	whom
	which	which
	that	that
	those	those
	these	these
Indefinite	anyone	anyone
	somebody	somebody
	each	each
	both	both
	few	few
	one	one
Reflexive	(no subjective form)	myself
		itself
		yourself
		herself
		himself
		ourselves
		yourselves
		themselves
Demonstrative	this	this
	that	that
	there	there
	these	these
	those	those

Interrogative	who	whom
	what	what
	which	which
	whose	whose
Possessive	mine	mine
	yours	yours
	its	its
	ours	ours
	yours	yours
	theirs	theirs
	his	his
	hers	hers

Pronouns are used in sentences just as nouns are (see p. 249).

VERBS

A verb is a word that expresses an action or state of being. It has many forms but is identified by its infinitive; e.g., to write, to listen, to be.

— She *wrote* the letter.
— Mr. Allen *listens* to the complaint.
— My assistant *is* efficient.

The **tense** of a verb indicates the time that the action or state of being takes place.

Present tense	— I *am* working.
Past tense	— I *was* working.
Future tense	— I *shall be* working.
Present perfect tense	— I *have been* working.
Past perfect tense	— I *had been* working.
Future perfect tense	— I *shall have been* working.

(Note: A verb in any tense other than the present tense requires a helper verb, called an auxiliary verb. "Shall" and "have" are auxiliaries of the verb "work" in the sentences above.)

The **voice** of a verb indicates the relationship between the verb and its subject.

• When the subject of the sentence is the doer of the action, the verb is in the **active voice**.
—Henry *set* a new sales record.

- When the subject of the sentence receives the action, the verb is in the **passive voice**. The passive voice always includes a form of the verb to be (e.g., am, was, been) as an auxiliary verb.

— I *was given* some drafting equipment by my supervisor. (Note: It is best to use the active voice as much as possible. For instance, the sentence above could be changed to "My supervisor *gave* me some drafting equipment." Messages expressed in the active voice tend to be clearer and more direct.)

ADJECTIVES

An adjective is a word used to describe a noun or pronoun.

— *His* instructions were *clear* and *complete*.

There are several kinds of adjectives:

Proper (formed from a proper noun)
— Most *French* people love music.
Demonstrative (answers "which one?")
— He prefers *that* computer.
Descriptive (answers "what kind?")
— They ordered *black* paint.
Qualitative (answers "how much?")
— He took a *little* money.
Possessive (answers "whose?")
— I used *his* desk.
Quantitative (answers "how many?")
— She takes *two* apples.
Note: **Indefinite** adjectives are used when this cannot be answered; e.g., "He took *some* samples."

Most adjectives have three different forms that are used to compare persons and things.

Positive —	small	good	unusual
Comparative —	smaller	better	more unusual
Superlative —	smallest	best	most unusual

— My report is *good*. His report is *better*. Your report is *best*.

ADVERBS

An adverb is a word that describes a verb, an adjective, or another adverb.

— The man walked *slowly*. (verb)
— The sky was *very* black. (adjective)
— He left town *too* quickly. (adverb)

There are several types of adverbs:

Adverbs of
manner answer "how?"
— She works *energetically.*
time answer "when?"
— It will be ready *soon.*
place answers "where?"
— They went *out.*
degree answers "to what extent?"
— He is *extremely* fast.

Interrogative adverbs introduce questions.
— *When* did you go?

Relative adverbs introduce clauses.
— I will meet you *when* I am finished work.

Conjunctive adverbs join two independent clauses.
— He liked the machine; *however,* he didn't buy it.

Many adverbs can be used in comparisons, just as adjectives are.
Positive — Ann checks her work *carefully.*
Comparative — Ann checks her work *more carefully.*
Superlative — Ann checks her work *most carefully.*

PREPOSITIONS
A preposition is the word that introduces a phrase. A phrase is a
small group of words (as few as two) including the preposition and a
noun or pronoun.
— *in* here
— *below* the stairs
Listed below are some common prepositions:

at	up	from	upon	below	beside	against	across
in	to	into	with	after	within	through	down
by	on	like	past	above	before	around	until
					under	between	over

(Note: To be a preposition, the word must be followed by a noun or
a pronoun; for example, "He went *before* the judge." In the
following sentence "before" is an adverb. "I never saw him
before.")

CONJUNCTIONS
A conjunction joins words, phrases, clauses, or sentences.
— The woman *and* the man are equally well qualified.
— They went into the room *but* not over to the table.
— He wants to know when you will go *and* how you will pay
for the trip.

There are three kinds of conjunctions:

Co-ordinating conjunctions join word groups of equal value—words with words or clauses with clauses.
— We will play basketball *or* baseball.
Subordinating conjunctions join subordinate clauses to the main clause.
— Finish your homework *if* you want to go out.
Correlative conjunctions are two conjunctions used as a pair.
— I had *neither* the time *nor* the patience to listen to her.

ARTICLES
The words "a," "an," and "the" are articles. They introduce nouns.
A boy wants to go home.
The team won.

PHRASES
A phrase is a group of words that forms a unit but that does not contain a verb.
He went *to the office*.
The manager, *unhappy with her work*, fired her.

CLAUSES
A clause is a group of words that contains a verb but is not a complete thought.
They chose our bid, *because we quoted the lowest price*.
The report *which I recommended* was finally chosen.

COMMON ERRORS IN GRAMMAR AND USAGE

SENTENCE ERRORS
Every grammatically complete sentence must have a subject (a noun or a pronoun) and a verb.
— We   must increase profits.
(subject)(verb)

The Sentence Fragment
When you are editing your written work, be on the look-out for incomplete sentences (fragments). A sentence fragment is a group of words that is missing either a subject or a complete verb.
— I didn't want to go. Having been there already.
(The last "sentence" is incomplete. It lacks a subject.)

— She always leaves early. A fine thing!
(The last "sentence" here is also incomplete. It lacks a verb.
Sometimes we use sentence fragments for emphasis—but use them
sparingly.)

The Run-on Sentence

This error is usually the result of faulty punctuation. Two complete
sentences are sometimes incorrectly separated by a comma rather
than a period.

   — I wanted to stay, my assistant didn't want to.

   Run-on sentences sometimes contain no punctuation whatsoever.

   — I attended that meeting and she was there and she took up
everybody's time with her long-winded ideas.
(Note: Words like "and" and "but" must never be used in place of a
period.)

SUBJECT-VERB AGREEMENT

Every subject and verb in every sentence must agree in number. If
the subject is singular, the verb must be singular. A plural subject
requires a plural verb.

   You would probably never write "He go to the bank" but you
might write "The president as well as her staff, have arrived." Since
"president" (singular) is the subject of this sentence, the verb must
be "*has* arrived."

   Note these examples:

   — She or Mary have the manual. (*incorrect*)
   — She or Mary has the manual. (*correct*)
   — Five hundred dollars were offered as a reward. (*incorrect*)
   — Five hundred dollars was offered as a reward. (*correct*)
   — Neither of us were criticized for being late. (*incorrect*)
   — Neither of us was criticized for being late. (*correct*)

PROBLEMS WITH PRONOUNS

Who/Whom

In colloquial language, many people say incorrectly, "Who did you
give that to?" In business writing, the correct use of "who" and
"whom" is expected.

   Correction: To whom did you give that?

   If you review the uses of pronouns, you will notice that they can
be either the subject of a sentence or the object of a verb or
preposition.

   — *Who* is going?
(subject)

— *Whom* did he hire?
(object of the verb)
— From *whom* did you get that book?
(object of the preposition "from")

Pronoun and Antecedent Agreement
The antecedent of a pronoun is the noun which the pronoun represents. Every pronoun must have an antecedent.
— Mr. Webber wants to resign because *he* is not well. (*correct*)
—She went to the store but *it* was too expensive. (*incorrect— missing antecedent*)
— John told his father that his car wouldn't start. (*confusion with antecedent — whose car?*)

Every pronoun must match or agree with its antecedent in number and in person.
— The *members* of the committee expressed *their* approval.
— *Everyone* should put on *her* or *his* coat.
— *One* of the cartons was lying on *its* side.

Troubles with Adjectives and Adverbs
Be very careful in your use of adjectives and adverbs. Remember that adjectives can only describe nouns. Adverbs describe verbs, adjectives, and other adverbs.
— He types good. (*incorrect—An adjective, "good," cannot describe a verb, "type."*)
He types real well. (*incorrect—an adjective, "real," cannot describe an adverb, "well."*)
— He types really well. (*correct*)
— His typing is very good. (*correct*)

PUNCTUATION
The purpose of punctuation is to help make the meaning of a written message clearer.
Consider the following five sentences. Changing the punctuation marks alters the meaning.

— Mary thought Jerry typed quickly.
— Mary thought; Jerry typed quickly,
— Mary thought Jerry typed quickly?
— Mary thought, "Jerry typed quickly!"
— "Mary," thought Jerry, "typed quickly!"

Punctuation marks are the traffic signals of writing; they help the reader move smoothly through your work. Try to think of punctuation not as a series of rules but rather as one way of making your message clear.

PERIOD .

Use a period:

• at the end of an imperative or declarative sentence or an indirect question.
 — The office manager is out right now.
 — Send us your cheque today.
 — Please speak up.
 — He asked if I was going.

• with abbreviations.
 — Dr. Ingard
 — Alta.

Note: When abbreviations become acronyms (a word formed from the first letters of each part of a long name or term), periods are omitted.
 — CARE
 — CIDA

QUESTION MARK ?

Use a question mark:

• at the end of direct questions.
 — Why did you order this much paper?
 — The boss wants to see me?

• to indicate doubt about some fact
 — Roger Bacon, 1214(?)–1294

EXCLAMATION MARK !

Use an exclamation mark:

• to indicate strong emotion or feeling such as surprise, delight, or excitement. The exclamation mark is almost never used in formal business writing. With the exception of advertising, where they are used more frequently, exclamation marks are used in informal communication only on those rare occasions when you wish to give a statement particular emphasis.
 — Last year our sales hit a record high — over one million dollars!

COLON :

Use a colon:

• after a complete sentence that is followed by a list.
—People carry many things in their briefcases: reports, newspapers, and brown-bag lunches.

• after the salutation in some business letters.
— Dear Sir or Madam:
— Dear Ms. Williams:

• when typing reference initials. The colon precedes the typist's initials.
— :mh

• to separate hours and minutes, parts of a ratio, parts of biblical citations, and parts of a book's title.
— 9:30 a.m.
— 20:1
— Luke 3:1
— Software: An Overview

• to introduce a direct quotation.
—The leaders at the business conference repeated their plea: "Lower taxes or lose your tax base."

SEMICOLON ;

Use a semicolon:

• between equal parts of a compound sentence when they are not joined by *and*, *but*, *nor*, or *or*.
— I want to finish the report now; I'll go for lunch later.
— For five days he looked for a job; by the sixth day he was very discouraged.

• to separate two independent clauses when the second clause is introduced by such words as *however, moreover, consequently, therefore, nevertheless, furthermore, besides,* and *instead.*
— Today is a holiday; therefore, the mail will not be delivered.
— He brought in coffee; however, nobody drank any.

• to emphasize a break between closely related clauses when one clause is long or when one clause already contains commas.
—Many common English surnames were created from personal characteristics, such as Little, Small, and Young; from locations, such as Hill, Brooks, and Wood; and from occupations, such as Baker, Miller, Shepherd, and Weaver.

—Dick is preparing the draft of the report; Joanne is typing the tables, charts, and graphs; and Eric is proofreading the completed pages.

COMMA   ,
Use a comma:
• before the conjunctions *and*, *but*, *or*, or *nor* in compound sentences where there are different subjects.
—The sales representative called several times, but the manager refused to see him.

• between words, phrases, or clauses in a series.
—The speaker carried her hat, coat, gloves, and a briefcase.
—I typed the pages, he made the copies, and she stapled them together.

• after introductory words, phrases, and clauses.
—Well, you can go this time.
—In making his decision, the president weighed all factors.
—Because her letter of application was neatly typed, I granted her an interview.

• to set off phrases that are not essential to the meaning of the sentence (appositives).
—Mr. Garcia, the office manager, is well organized.
—The vice-president, jubilant at our increase in profits, promised us a bonus.

• to show the omission of a verb.
—Her typing was inaccurate; her desk, disorganized; and her work, messy.

• to set off the name of a person being addressed.
—Mrs. LeRoy, your efforts are greatly appreciated.

• to set off parts of a date.
—By March 11, 1988, all accounts will be closed.

• to set off parts of an address or geographical location.
—Our office is located at 5615 Elm Street, Calgary, Alta.
—Mr. I.M. Incharge,
  The Busy Bee Company,
  44 Main Street,
  Beautiful, Province
  B2S 1K0

• after the salutation and complimentary closing in some business letters.
— Dear Karen,
— Yours sincerely,

• to set off a quotation from the rest of the sentence.
—"I hope," John mused, "that there are no more rules for the comma."

APOSTROPHE   '
Use an apostrophe:
• to show possession.
— That is Odette's desk.
— This is the women's coatroom.
— The boys' team won.
— I like Keats' poems.
Note: In cases where the word ends with "s," the general rule is to add only the apostrophe.

• to indicate that a letter or letters have been omitted (contractions).
— I am   I'm
— It is   It's
— she will   she'll
— they are   they're

HYPHEN -
Use a hyphen:
• to divide a word at the end of a line when there is not enough space for the whole word. Always place the hyphen at the end of the line, never at the beginning of the next line.
—We had so much business that we could not pass the amend-ment.
(a) Divide compound words between their parts,
     — moon-light
(b) Divide a word by syllables,
     — iden-tify
(c) Divide an already hyphenated word only at the existing hyphen.
     — twenty-dollar (not twenty-dol-lar)
     — self-respect (not self-re-spect)

(d) Divide between double consonants.
  — bab-ble
  — run-ning
  But divide after double consonants if the root word ends in the double consonant.
— pull-ing
— miss-ing
(e) Do not divide or hyphenate proper names, sums of money, numbers, time, contractions, abbreviations, or acronyms.
— 3 416 521   (not 3 416-521)
— Mr. Jones   (not Mr. -Jones)
— $50,000   (not $50,-000)
— 8:30 a.m.   (not 8:30 -a.m.)
— shouldn't   (not should-n't)
— UNICEF   (not UNI-CEF)
Note: There are some exceptions to these rules. Check your dictionary whenever you are unsure about hyphenating words.

• to join two or more words to form compound adjectives which precede the noun they modify.
— up-to-date merchandise
— well-stocked supply cupboard
Note: When the same words follow a noun, do not hyphenate.
— This file is up to date.
— That store is always well stocked.

• to avoid the awkward doubling of vowels.
— semi-independence
— re-elect

• when spelling out compound numbers between 21 and 99.
— sixty-one
— twenty-ninth

• with "ex," "self," and "elect."
— ex-president
— self-righteous
— premier-elect

DASH —
Note: To indicate a dash, use one line (–)when writing and two hyphens when typing. (--)
Use a dash:
• to indicate a sudden change or break in thought.
—The best way to finish that—but no, you don't want my opinion.

• before a repeated word or expression or to link an added comment to the main idea of the sentence.
—I want him fired—fired for his disloyalty.

• to emphasize part of a sentence.
—Ellie Tramoli—the woman we met earlier today—has been promoted to assistant manager.

• before a summarizing statement introduced by words such as all or this.
—Fame, fortune, and status—these are the rewards of hard work.

PARENTHESES (   )
Use parentheses:
• to enclose a reference to a period of time.
—He lived a long time (1610–1693).

• to express an amount of money when more than one dollar is indicated.
—The bill from the attorney was for five hundred dollars ($500).

• around numbers or letters that indicate subdivisions of a sentence.
—Our three aims are: (1) to increase sales, (2) to reduce expenses, and (3) to retain all our employees.

• to enclose an explanation, example, or qualification.
—His latest plan (according to his assistant) is to apply for more money.
—Shakespeare's most difficult tragedy (*Hamlet*) has never been performed by this company of actors.

BRACKETS [   ]
Use brackets:
• for comment or explanation which is inserted in a quotation.
—He wrote the president of our company: "What you have suggested [that we have not paid our account] is absolutely without foundation."

• to insert explanatory material inside a set of parentheses to avoid confusion.

—His latest plan (according to his assistant [the nephew of the boss]) is to apply for more money.

QUOTATION MARKS " "
Use quotation marks:
• to enclose a direct quotation (the exact words of the speaker).
  — He said, "You know you're right."
  — "You know," he said, "you're right."
  — "You know you're right," he said.

Note: When the quotation is a complete sentence, the comma and periods go inside the closing quotation mark. When it is not a complete sentence, the punctuation goes outside the closing quotation marks. However, in printed books, including this one, commas and periods are always placed *inside* closing quotation marks for aesthetic purposes. Other punctuation follows the rule above.
  —The first report, "Daycare in the Workplace," was well received.

• to single out or emphasize words of particular importance. (This should be used sparingly).
  — On Bay Street, a "hot issue" is a new stock that rises sharply.

• to set off the names of chapters of books, radio and television programs, and articles in magazines.
  — "The Business of Listening"
  — "The Journal"
  — "How to Buy a Disk Drive"

Note: Titles of books, magazines, and newspapers are underlined or italicized.

• Single quotation marks are used for a quotation within a quotation.
  — "He asked me to read 'The Business of Speaking'," she said.

CAPITALIZATION
Knowing when to use capital letters can sometimes be confusing. The following general rules will help you. Capitalize:

• the first word of a complete sentence, and of a quoted sentence.
  — He went to work.
  — Mary asked, "Can Jerry type?"

- proper names and their abbreviations.
  - France
  - Sir John A. Macdonald
  - R.C.M.P.
  - B.A.

- titles when they come before the person's name but not after.
  - Governor Laura Bradley
  - Laura Bradley, the governor of our college

- the names and abbreviations of businesses, industries, agencies, schools, political parties, and religious denominations.
  - J & S Manufacturing
  - the Canada Council
  - Timothy Eaton Secondary School

- the names of specific branches, departments, and other divisions of government.
  - House of Commons
  - the Ministry of Labour
  - the Supreme Court

- the names of weekdays, months, holidays, and other special days or periods. (Use lower-case for the seasons of the year.)
  - Tuesday
  - June
  - Christmas Eve
  - National Book Week
  - fall, winter, spring, summer

- the important words in the salutation but only the first word of the complimentary close of a letter.
  - Dear Sir or Madam:
  - Yours sincerely,

- the specific part of the trade name of a product.
  - Kraft dinner
  - Levi's jeans

- the first and last words and all other words except articles, prepositions, and co-ordinate conjunctions in the titles of books, periodicals, articles, and reports.
  - The Business of English
  - The Wall Street Journal
  - The Need for Staff Re-location: a Report

NUMBERS

TWO NUMBERS TOGETHER
- Use commas in lists of numbers.
— The winning numbers were 27, 29, and 300.

- Spell the smaller of two numbers appearing together when one is a compound modifier.
  — They read 3 two-volume books.
  — He bought 2 three-piece suits.

NUMBERS ABOVE TEN
- Use figures.
  — 15 acres, 100 hectares, 10 000 cars, $5,000
(The International System of Units omits the comma and for numbers above 9999 inserts a space instead of a comma, except for amounts of money.)

NUMBERS UNDER TEN
- Spell these numbers.
— I sold three rowing machines today.
— There were ten minutes left in the game.
Note: If a sentence contains numbers above and below ten, be consistent.
— The company delivered ten telephones to this branch office and fifty to the office in Montreal.
— The company returned 6 telephones and kept 44 others.

NUMBERS BEGINNING A SENTENCE
- The number should be spelled out.
— Twenty-five tickets were sold.

FRACTIONS
- Write a fraction in words when it stands alone.
  — The sisters ate two-thirds of the pizza.

- A whole number with a fraction is written in numbers.
  — Together the brothers ate 9½ chickens.

MONEY
- Use numbers and the word "cents" for amounts under one dollar.
— The chocolate bar cost 65 cents.

- Use the dollar sign ($) and numbers for amounts of one dollar or more.
— The poster cost $9.98.

- Omit cents for even dollar amounts.
— The most popular poster cost $10 last week.

NUMBERS FOLLOWING A NOUN
- Use numbers after the noun.
 — Size 5, Model 253, Room 8
 — Serial No. 7890

PER CENT
- Use "per cent" unless it is contained in technical material.
—Almost 60 per cent of those surveyed agreed with making laws tougher for those who drink and drive.

HOUSE NUMBERS
- House number one is spelled out.
— One Castlemere Crescent

- Streets with a number between one and ten for their name are spelled out.
— The head office is on Seventh Avenue.
— They live at 224 East 52nd Street.

TIME
- The 12-hour clock uses numbers before a.m. and p.m.
— School starts at 8:45 a.m.

- The 24-hour clock always uses four numbers.
— School starts at 0845 and ends at 1530.

DATES
- For numeric dates, use eight figures for year, month, and day.
— 1987 03 13 (March 13, 1987)

- For non-numeric, use figures for the day and the year.
— February 12, 1943

- Use st, th, nd, and rd when the day precedes the month.
— the 1st of July.
— the 6th of August.

FREQUENTLY MISSPELLED WORDS

A
absence
access
accommodate
accumulate
acknowledge
addressed
adjourn
all right
anxious
appropriate
association

B
believed
benefited
beneficial
budgeted

C
calculation
cannot
certificate
column
coming
commit
commitment
committed
companies
components
conscious
correspondence
credible

D
debt
decision
develop
difference
dilemma

E
efficiency
elementary
eliminated
emphasis
enough
equipped
essential
exaggerate
excellent
executive
exercise

F
familiar
February
financial
formula

G
genuine
government
grievance
guarantee

H
height
honorary
hurriedly
humorous

I
immediately
independence
institute
interpret
interrupt
irrelevant

K
knowledge

L
legitimate
liaison

M
maintenance
manufacture
mechanism
miscellaneous
municipal

N
necessary
negotiate
neither
ninety
ninth

O
obsolete
occasion
occur
occurrence
omission
omit
omitted
organization

P
parallel
particular
perceive
perseverance
precise
preference
procedure

R
really
received

S
safety
scarcely
schedule
separate
shipment
shipped
significant
similar
strictly
superintendent
symptom
synchronize

T
technique
transferred
trivial

U
unanimous
undoubtedly
unnecessary

V
valuable
vertical
view

W
waive
Wednesday
whatever
whether
written

Y
younger
youth

Z
zealous
zoology

regulation
relevant
replies

13   12   9   15   1

COMMON MIX-UPS

a lot	a great deal	A lot of people work in that department.
allot	distribute	Her job is to allot the budget money.
accept	to take delivery of	He accepted the shipment.
except	not including	Everyone except the manager went to the seminar.
affect	verb — to influence	How will this affect delivery?
effect	noun — result	The effect of the advertising campaign was significant.
bases	plural of base or basis	That corporation has several international bases.
basis	foundation, reason	These studies form the basis of her report.
complement	to make complete	That tie complements your outfit.
compliment	praise	He is very complimentary about our staff.
council	assembly of people	The city council will vote on that tonight.
counsel	advice	She is an expert at career counselling.
dual	double, composed of two parts	This is a dual control airplane.
duel	fight between two people	He was challenged to a duel.
it's	contraction of it is, it has	It's time to go to work.
its	shows ownership	Its price was too high.
licence	noun	He is applying for his driver's licence.
license	verb	She works for the Licensing Commission.
loose	not fastened completely	That wire is loose.
lose	become unable to find	When did you lose your wallet?

passed	from verb "to pass"	The deadline for applications has passed.
past	beyond, time gone by	Her office is just past the lobby.
personal	one's own	He made a lot of personal calls from work.
personnel	staff	There is a low turnover of personnel in that company.
peruse	study carefully	He perused the financial report for hours.
pursue	follow, continue	She pursued the issue of shorter working hours with her supervisor.
practice	noun	He has started his own law practice.
practise	verb	He has been practising his typing.
precede	go before	These are the work orders for this week and the two preceding weeks.
proceed	go further, continue	Please proceed with your work.
principal	most important, head	She is the principal shareholder in our company.
principle	rule, law	Customer satisfaction is the guiding principle of this firm.
quiet	not noisy	I prefer to work in a quiet office.
quite	actually, really	This job will be quite a change for them.
stationary	not moving	That built-in equipment is stationary.
stationery	writing, office supplies	She has engraved stationery.
than	used in comparison	Your report is better than mine.
then	at that time, next	Will it be ready then?
there	in that place	Put the files in there.
their	shows ownership	My neighbours sold their house.
they're	contraction of they are	They're going to buy some shares.

thorough	attentive to detail	She checked the figures thoroughly.
through	from end to end	Go through the office to the warehouse.
to	in the direction of	I would rather go to the Board Meeting.
too	also, more than enough	She worked on the report too.
two	number	She has two job interviews.
who's	contraction of who is, who has	Who's going to answer the door?
whose	shows ownership	Whose coat is this?
your	shows ownership	This is your desk.
you're	contraction of you are	You're going to like your new boss.
between	refers to two people or things	He sat between the desk and the table.
among	refers to two or more people or things	The nurse went among the sick children in the ward.
can	be able to	I can drive a car.
may	be permitted to	I will ask if I may drive her car.
good	adjective	His good manners are appreciated.
well	adverb	We work well together.
in	within a place	The files are in the cabinet.
into	from outside to inside	She walked into the wrong room.

PROOFREADER'S MARKS

Symbol	Meaning	Example
#	indent # spaces	② She had two jobs.
⌐	move right	Nobody wanted the job.
⌐	move left	She did not type well.
][or ctr	centre	Common Mix-ups
¶	paragraph	¶ He did not hesitate to answer.
no ¶	no paragraph	no ¶ Taxes were increased then.
☰	capitalize	They loved canadian winters.
☰	all capitals	My Summer Vacation
/ lc	lower case	They enjoyed each other's Company.
◡	close up space	This is re ally good.
ℓ	delete word	This is for the the office.
ℓ	delete letter	They ate tooo much food.
ℐ	delete and close up	That is uttterly ridiculous.
#	insert space	Themeeting is important.
⌃	insert comma	She wanted knives, forks, and spoons.
⌄	insert apostrophe	The Presidents car arrived.
⌄ ⌄	insert quotation marks	She said, I appreciate that.
⊙	insert period	The order was delayed three days.
⊙	insert colon	Order the following items.
⌃;	insert semi-colon	He will do it however, he'll be late.
/=	insert hyphen	He wore up to date clothes. /= /=
/--	insert dash	Eat well cheese, milk, fruits. /--
⌐	insert material in margin	We must go the meeting now. /to
∿ or trs	transpose	We gave him hte book.
sp	spell in full	He lives on Seventh Ave. sp
··· or stet	let it stand	He is always late for work. stet

STANDARD ABBREVIATIONS

CANADIAN PROVINCES AND TERRITORIES:

Alberta	Alta.	AB
British Columbia	B.C.	BC
Manitoba	Man.	MB
New Brunswick	N.B.	NB
Newfoundland	Nfld.	NF
Northwest Territories	N.W.T.	NT
Nova Scotia	N.S.	NS
Ontario	Ont.	ON
Prince Edward Island	P.E.I.	PE
Québec	P.Q.	PQ
Saskatchewan	Sask.	SK
Yukon Territories	Y.T.	YT

AMERICAN STATES:

Alabama	Ala.	AL
Alaska	Alas.	AK
Arizona	Ariz.	AZ
Arkansas	Ark.	AR
California	Calif.	CA
Colorado	Colo.	CO
Connecticut	Conn.	CT
Delaware	Del.	DE
District of Columbia	D.C.	DC
Florida	Fla.	FL
Georgia	Ga.	GA
Hawaii	Hawaii	HI
Idaho	Ida.	ID
Illinois	Ill.	IL
Indiana	Ind.	IN
Iowa	Iowa	IA
Kansas	Kans.	KS
Kentucky	Ky.	KY
Louisiana	La.	LA
Maine	Me.	ME
Maryland	M.D.	MD
Massachusetts	Mass.	MA
Michigan	Mich.	MI
Minnesota	Minn.	MN
Mississippi	Miss.	MS
Missouri	Mo.	MO
Montana	Mont.	MT

Nebraska	Nebr.	NE
Nevada	Nev.	NV
New Hampshire	N.H.	NH
New Jersey	N.J.	NJ
New Mexico	N.Mex.	NM
New York	N.Y.	NY
North Carolina	N.C.	NC
North Dakota	N.Dak.	ND
Ohio	Ohio	OH
Oklahoma	Okla.	OK
Oregon	Oreg.	OR
Pennsylvania	Penn.	PA
Rhode Island	R.I.	RI
South Carolina	S.C.	SC
South Dakota	S.Dak.	SD
Tennessee	Tenn.	TN
Texas	Tex.	TX
Utah	Utah	UT
Vermont	Vt.	VT
Virginia	Va.	VA
Washington	Wash.	WA
West Virginia	W.Va.	WV
Wisconsin	Wis.	WI
Wyoming	Wyo.	WY

THE POSTAL CODE

A postal code always consists of six characters—letter, number, letter, space, number, letter, number. It should always be the last line on the envelope. Do not underline it or place a period after it.

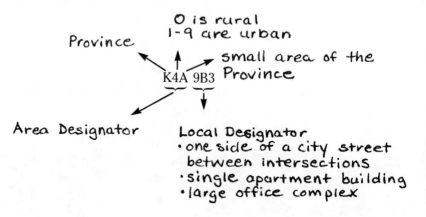

The postal code is an important component of the mechanized processing systems being used by more and more post offices around the world. At Canada Post, for example, an Optical Character Reader (OCR), working at a speed of approximately 30 000 pieces of mail per hour, automatically reads the Postal Code in the address and translates it into computer readable bar codes. These bar codes are then sprayed on the envelope with phosphorescent ink (yellow or orange).

The OCR is only able to read the Postal Code if it is in the correct place on the envelope and has been typed or in some way mechanically printed. Handwritten codes are rejected by the OCR and are sent to a department where the phosphorescent bar codes are keypunched on to each envelope.

All letters with bar codes go to a letter sorting machine which can sort approximately 20 000 pieces per hour. Letters without any postal code have to be sorted manually—a process which takes much longer.

GLOSSARY

GLOSSARY

abstract

A term used to describe ideas and qualities which are general, rather than specific. The opposite of **concrete**. For example, photography is abstract; a photograph is concrete. [*see: concrete*]

acronym

A name made from the first letters of a series of words (e.g., SCUBA — sealed circuit underwater breathing apparatus).

advancement (opportunity for)

In any job interview, try to identify what the chances are of your receiving promotion within the firm or business. Even if the likelihood of such advancement is small, don't necessarily refuse a job offer — it may provide just the experience you need to move on to bigger and better things with a different company in the future.

agenda

Most formal business meetings — and some informal ones — will have an agenda. This is a list of the topics which are to be discussed at the meeting, and is generally sent to participants well in advance of the meeting so that they are able to prepare any necessary material.

amendment

In a formal business meeting, decisions are made by all participants voting to accept (or defeat) a motion. A motion can be altered, or amended, during the discussion which precedes the vote. When an amendment to a motion is passed, it means that the original motion (e.g., "to accept the executive director's resignation") is lost, and it is the amended motion ("to accept the executive director's resignation only when we have hired a replacement for her") which is put to the vote. [*see: motion*]

annual general meeting

Most corporations which have shareholders, and charitable (and other) organizations which have general members, are required by law to hold a meeting of shareholders/members once every calendar year. One of the major purposes of such a meeting is that each voting member of the organization is able to express her/his opinion of the actions of the officers/directors during the previous year.

annual report

A company with shareholders is required by law to publish a yearly outline of the financial performance of the company. This can vary from a few, to hundreds of pages in length depending on the size and scope of the company's operations. The Annual Report is usually distributed to shareholders 30–60 days before the Annual General Meeting.

appearance

How you dress and care for your personal appearance is important both at a job interview and on the job. Employers very often have limited time to spend interviewing and have to make very quick judgements. Dress carefully and appropriately. [see: body language; dress code]

article

a) A part of speech — the words "a," "an," and "the."
b) A piece of writing such as you would read in a magazine or newspaper. [see: feature article]

attitude

The way you approach:
a) sending and receiving messages
b) finding a job
In either case your attitude must be positive. [see: objective; subjective]

audience

The receiver of your message—it may be one person, or it may be many. The more you know about your audience, the more effective your communication is likely to be. [see: communication, level of language]

audio system

Some meetings, and some presentations, require the use of an audio system which could be as simple as a single microphone used by all speakers, or could be far more complex, involving a number of input sources. If you are responsible for a meeting or presentation involving any kind of audio system make sure you know beforehand how it all works, or have someone with you who does.

automated office, the

Sometimes referred to as the office of the future—but it is here now. As computers become smaller and more efficient; as the

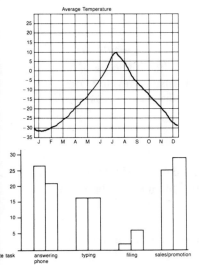

possibilities of world-wide electronic communications expand; the automated office becomes more and more of a reality.

axis graph
Where two quantities are plotted one against the other along a common axis. [*see: graph*]

bar graph
Similar to an axis graph, a bar graph shows a measured quantity (e.g., population) in relation to one or more descriptive factors or groups (e.g. the provinces of Canada) which are represented by bars. [*see: graph*]

barrier to communication
Anything which prevents a message from being "received and understood." It can be caused by either the receiver or the sender of a message, and might be something as simple as the receiver having a radio playing too loudly while trying to listen to your message.

bibliography
A list of sources—books, magazines, films, etc.—used to research material for a report. It is normally included as the last page of a report. [*see: formal report*]

body (formal report)
The body (major part) of a **formal report** includes the *purpose* (why the report was written); the *method* (how the necessary information was gathered); the *findings* (what this information proved); and the *conclusions* (what should/should not be done as a result of this information).

body (informal report)
In an **informal report**, the body (the major part) is made up of all the facts (the considerations) which back up the recommendations and conclusions. [*see: conclusion; recommendations*]

body language
A form of non-verbal communication. [*see: appearance; distancing; eye contact; facial expression; gestures; posture*]

by-law
A rule or regulation which concerns how a company is run. A by-law will, for example, outline the duties and responsibilities of the officers (Board of Directors, etc.) of the company. [*see: constitution*]

cause and effect

A method of organizing the content of a message which gives the reasons for and results of an action (e.g., "Because of last night's snow storm [*cause*], all public transit is running late and many employees will probably be late for work [*effect*]". [*see: organizer*]

chairperson

The person in charge of any meeting. In a formal meeting the chairperson is referred to in the third person as "the chair."

charts

Visual aids, used in the course of a presentation, or in the body of a report, to make potentially confusing material clearer. For example, lists of numbers are often easier for listeners to understand if they can *see* them as well.

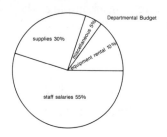

circle (pie) graph

A graph in which the 360° of a circle are divided proportionately by degrees to represent a desired commodity. For example, you might draw a circle graph representing your day as: 8 hours sleep (120°), 8 hours school (120°), and 8 hours recreation (120°). [*see: graph*]

clarity

Part of voice control. The clarity with which you speak has a tremendous effect on how well your message is received and understood. If you leave endings off words, for example, or run your words together, your listeners will be too busy puzzling out what you're trying to say, to "get the message." [*see: voice control*]

cliché

An expression or phrase that has been used so often it is no longer effective (e.g., "new and improved").

collage

A picture made by using a variety of photographs, pieces of writing, and just about anything else you can think of. [*see: juxtaposition*]

collection letters

Letters sent by companies in an effort to collect payment of overdue accounts. The initial collection letter will probably be fairly mild; after several unsuccessful efforts to collect from a customer, a company may resort to legal action.

colloquial language

Oral (spoken) language of a very informal nature. It is never acceptable in written business communications, and seldom acceptable in spoken business communications. [*see: level of language*]

colloquialism

An informal phrase or expression which is perfectly acceptable in colloquial language (e.g., "I'm hitting the books tonight!"). [*see colloquial language*]

communication

Communication occurs when a message sent is received. **Effective** communication occurs when the message sent is received **and understood**.

communication model, the

The communication model has five parts:

The **Sender** — the person who initiates communication.

The **Message** — what the sender wants to say.

The **Medium** — how the sender puts the message (letter, phone, etc.)

The **Receiver** — the person who "gets the message."

Feedback — the receiver's reaction to the message.

comparison/contrast

A method of organizing the content of a message. The merits and demerits of two or more items/ideas are placed side by side, and a final evaluation is made. In comparison, both similarities and differences are listed; in contrast, only the differences are listed. [*see: juxtaposition; organizer*]

computer graphics

Visual material such as charts and graphs produced and printed by computer. [*see: computer program*]

computer program

A series of coded instructions which control the operations of a computer. Different programs accomplish different functions — for example, one program will allow you to do word processing; another will enable the computer to perform accounting functions, etc.

conclusion

In the context of this text, the conclusion is the ending of any written or spoken communication. The conclusion very often summarizes everything that has been said in the message. In report writing, the conclusions are the deductions made on the basis of the information presented. [*see: formal report; informal report*]

concrete

Something which exists in a specific form (e.g., a photograph, a typewriter). [*see: abstract*]

consensus

When the majority of a group of people agree as to their opinion of any subject, they are said to have reached a consensus.

constitution

The record of bylaws and principles by which a company is run. The major purpose of the constitution is to protect the shareholders of the company. [*see: bylaw*]

content

The information or what is said in any message, be it verbal or non-verbal. [*see: audience; purpose*]

context

The ideas, words, and phrases which surround an individual word. By examining these, you will very often be able to decide on the meaning of a word you do not at first understand.

co-operative education job

Many school boards run co-operative education programs in which a student will spend part of her or his school time in class, and part in a work placement, learning "on the job."

copyright

Any piece of creative work—written, artistic, performed, computer software, etc.—is protected by copyright laws and cannot be reproduced without the permission of the author or the copyright holder (not necessarily the same person). [*see: plagiarize*]

data

Facts or information. (N.B. the word is plural, and must always be accompanied by a plural verb—"*the data are . . .*" not "*the data is . . .*")

decision-making process

A series of steps which must be followed by a corporation (or a committee) before agreement as to a particular course of action is reached. The decision-making process will vary from company to company. For example, in a very large company all major decisions will probably be made by the Board of Directors; in a small company, decisions will probably be made by the owner (or manager), possibly in consultation with senior staff.

dialogue

The written form of a conversation between two or more people.

distancing

The space you place between yourself and the person/people to whom you are talking. This space will vary according to the purpose of your conversation and could range from 15 cm to 4.5 m. [*see: body language*]

dress code

Some companies may have a list of suggestions as to what employees should or should not wear to work. A dress code normally is of benefit to both employer and employee, in that it creates a positive public image for the company. Dress codes are also used in some businesses for health and safety reasons. [*see: appearance*]

edit

To revise and improve a piece of writing—always remembering the Six Cs of business writing (Is it: complete, concise, courteous, correct, clear, creative?)

envelopes, printed

Most businesses—large or small—use envelopes on which the company name, address, and logo have been printed. [*see: logo*]

eye contact
When you are talking to one person, it is a good idea to look at her/his eyes as you speak (although not to such an extent that you make your listener uncomfortable). When you are talking to more than one person, look at each of your listeners—do not fix your eyes on one individual. [*see: body language*]

facial expression
The look on your face very often communicates your thoughts and feelings better than any words could. [*see: body language*]

feature article (newspaper)
The story accompanying the page one headline.

feedback
The response from the receiver of a message. Feedback may be verbal (e.g., "I don't understand") or non-verbal (e.g., a puzzled frown). [*see: communication model*]

fiber-optic phones
Telephones which use fiber-optics (the transmission of images through threads made of glass) instead of normal telephone cables to relay messages.

flow chart
A diagram which explains the sequence of steps in any activity.

form letter
A standard letter—very often a sales letter—sent to many different recipients. The content of each letter is the same, but it is made more personal by having each receiver's name and address on it. Often, too, the receiver will be mentioned by name at various points throughout the letter.

formal language
The level of language used in most written, and many spoken, business communications. The degree of formality can vary— a legal document will be very formal; a letter to a company customer will be less so. [*see: level of language*]

formal (long) report
A formal report follows a definite format, containing:
1. Title page
2. Letter of transmittal
3. Table of Contents
4. Preface

5. Summary
6. Body — purpose, method, findings, conclusion
7. Recommendations
8. Bibliography
[*see the individual entries for each in this glossary*]

format of message
The way in which you choose to organize your message within a particular medium. For example, you might decide that the best medium for your message is a written one; you might then choose to send it in the format of a formal business letter.

general to specific
A method of organizing the content of your message in which you begin with a general statement then add more specific details (e.g., "I don't like this job. The hours are too long and the salary is too low."). [*see: organizer*]

gestures
The way in which you use your hands as you speak often adds a great deal to non-verbal communication. [*see: body language*]

goals, career
Your plans for your career.
a) Immediate goals—what you would like to achieve in your job over the next year or two.
b) Long-range goals—what you would like to have achieved, five or ten years from now.

graph
A diagram showing the relationship between two or more variable quantities or qualities. [*see: axis graph; bar graph; circle graph*]

graphics
The use of diagrams to help explain an idea or concept which is difficult to clarify using words alone. [*see: computer graphics; non-verbal communication*]

hierarchy
The chain of command in any company or organization, arranged by degree of power or responsibility.

high profile job
A job which is constantly in the public eye (e.g., politician, T.V. newsreader).

homonym
A word which sounds the same as another, but has a different spelling and a different meaning. (e.g., hear, here)

index
An alphabetically arranged list, usually at the end of a book, of names, topics, etc., and the page numbers on which they occur. An index is a useful tool in research to help you decide whether a book contains the specific information you need.

informal language
The level of language—written and spoken—used by most people in their daily lives. It can vary from nearly formal (how you talk to your boss) to very informal (how you talk to your peers). [see: level of language]

informal (short) report
Normally written in the form of a memo, and follows a specific format:
    recommendations
    body (major considerations)
    conclusion
[see the individual entries for each in this glossary]

information
Ideas or facts that are known or communicated.

inter-office communications
The transmission of information between people in an office or company by telephone, personal note, or memorandum.

intonation
The pattern of the different sounds of your voice as you speak. [see: voice control]

introduction
a) An explanatory section at the beginning of a book which gives an idea of what the book is like.
b) The presentation of one person to another the first time they meet.

inventory
A detailed list of goods or products in a company or store. To take inventory means to count all the products and determine their value.

jargon

Specialized words or expressions used by a particular profession or group (e.g., scientists, musicians).

job leads

Possible means of finding work; may be *visible* (e.g., want ads, bulletin boards, or window signs) or *hidden* (e.g., friends and relatives, Yellow Pages).

job market, the

The opportunities for employment or the availability of work that exists at any given time.

job security

The probability that a job with a company will last and will not be lost due to automation or bad economic conditions in that field.

journal

A daily record of events and personal impressions.

juxtaposition

Putting two ideas or things beside each other, so that the differences or similarities between them are emphasized. [*see: collage; comparison/contrast*]

letter of transmittal

A letter to introduce a formal business report. It is used only when the report is sent to someone outside the company. [*see: formal report*]

letter to the editor

A letter to the editor of a newspaper or magazine, often to express an opinion about a previous article. These letters are published in a special section of the newspaper/magazine — usually a particular page on which nothing else is printed.

letterhead paper

Stationery on which a company's name, address, and telephone number are printed or engraved and which may also include a logo and telex numbers and cable address. [*see: logo*]

level of language

The type of speaking and writing suitable for different occasions. Levels of language range in formality; for example, the

language you use in business communications, both verbal
and written, is more formal than the language you use when
speaking to friends. Very formal language is generally used
only in written communications. [*see: audience; colloquial
language; formal language; informal language*]

logo

A symbol used to represent a business or organization. Often
the name or the initials of the company are incorporated into
the design.

magazine, professional

A specialized publication written for a specific audience and
covering a specific, generally "white-collar," occupation.

magazine, trade

A specialized publication written for a specific audience and
covering a specific, generally manual or "blue-collar,"
occupation.

main idea

The principal or most important piece of information in any
communication—verbal or non-verbal. Other information
may be included to explain or support the main idea.

manufacturing

An industry which uses machinery to produce its goods. [*see:
service business*]

medium

The means by which a message is transmitted (e.g., a picture,
a letter). plural: media [*see: communication model*]

meeting, formal

A meeting which is run according to strict procedures. [*see:
rules of order*]

meeting, informal

A meeting which may have some procedural guidelines but
does not have rules that are clearly defined and recorded. The
size and nature of the meeting as well as the participants
usually determine the level of formality.

memorandum or memo

An informal written message which is the most common

method for internal business communications. plural: memoranda [*see: inter-office communications; personal note*]

message
The idea or information transmitted by a *sender* to a *receiver*. [*see: communication model*]

microcomputer
A computer in which the central processor has an integrated chip which contains all the logic elements needed for a complete computer system.

minutes of a meeting
The official record of what happened at a meeting, prepared by the recording secretary and distributed to those who attended the meeting.

motion
A proposal that is to be discussed and voted on at a formal business meeting. [*see: amendment; voting*]

N/A (not applicable)
A notation to use when filling out forms, to indicate that you have not missed supplying information but that a particular section of the form does not apply to you.

non-verbal communication
Communication without words. [*see: body language; graphics; voice control*]

notice of meeting
A notice which states the time, date, place, and purpose of a formal business meeting and which must be sent to everyone who should or would want to attend.

objective
Being able to remain uninfluenced by personal opinions or feelings in any situation, including when sending or receiving messages.

optical character reader (OCR)
A machine which "reads" typewritten material and transfers it automatically onto computer disk. The post office uses an OCR to read the postal codes on envelopes and translate them into computer readable bar codes.

order of importance
A method of organizing your message, beginning with the most important fact and stating the following facts in decreasing order. [*see: organizer*]

organizer
A system or pattern for arranging objects or ideas into a particular order. [*see: cause and effect; comparison/contrast; general to specific; order of importance; pros and cons; simple listing; spatial order; time order*]

pace
The rate or speed at which something is done (e.g., speaking). [*see: voice control*]

part-time job
A job at which you work for only part of the working day or week. The maximum number of hours you are legally allowed to work in any one week and still be considered "part-time" is usually twenty-five.

peers
One who is the equal of others in rank or authority—your friends and classmates are your peers. [*see: subordinates*]

performance rating
Measures how well a specific task is done or the level of achievement for a certain skill.

permanent job
A job which may be full-time or part-time but which is not temporary or performed for a limited period of time.

personal data sheet
A record of personal information (e.g., parents' names and dates of birth; your postal code; etc.) which you will often find useful when filling out forms and job applications.

personal note
A handwritten notice, often on personalized stationery, to a co-worker. A personal note is more informal than a memorandum. [*see: inter-office communications; memorandum*]

pitch
How high or low your voice is. Pitch varies according to the tension of your vocal cords. [*see: voice control*]

plagiarize
To use someone else's ideas or words as your own, giving no credit or recognition to the original author. [*see: quotation*]

point of order
At a formal business meeting a point of order is a statement that the rules of order are being violated or a demand that the rules be followed. [*see: rules of order*]

post office box number
Part of a mailing address; a number used to identify a box at a post office where mail may be sent and picked up by the person or company which rents the box.

postal station name
Part of a mailing address, particularly in large cities where there may be more than one location at which mail is sorted (e.g., Postal Station C).

posture
The position in which you place your body when you stand or sit or walk. [*see: body language*]

preface
An introductory statement at the beginning of a book or report, telling you in a general way what the subject is that is being written about. [*see: formal report*]

presentation
An oral report, or speech, usually to more than one person and frequently involving the use of props. A presentation should have a definite beginning, middle, and conclusion. [*see: conclusion; props*]

primary information
First-hand information that you collect by doing original research (e.g., from interviews and questionnaires). [*see: secondary information*]

proofreader's marks
Standard symbols used to indicate corrections to be made to typed or written work.

proofreading
Reading and examining material to ensure it is correct.

propaganda
A communication which contains distorted information and which is intended to persuade, usually on an emotional basis.

props
Items used in a business (or any) presentation to add interest or help clarify information (e.g., charts, pictures, slides, etc.).

pros and cons
A method of organizing your message by presenting arguments in favour of (pro) and against (con) a certain idea or action. [*see: organizer*]

purchase orders
A verbal or, more usually, written request to a company to supply specific items.

purpose
The sender's reason for communicating.

qualitative
Able to be described in abstract terms (e.g., colour). [*see: abstract*]

quantitative
Able to be measured in concrete terms (e.g., height, weight). [*see: concrete*]

quotation
The exact words of a writer or speaker. When you use a quotation in any communication, you must credit (acknowledge) the source. [*see: plagiarize*]

reading rate
The speed at which you read. Reading rate depends on the importance of the message, the complexity of the material, and the level of language. [*see: proofreading; reading with concentration; skim-reading*]

reading with concentration
As used in this text, the term refers to the speed (rate) at which you read a particular piece of material. When you read with concentration, you usually read slowly, and are reading to understand and to retain information. [*see: reading rate; skim-reading*]

receiver

The person who hears, reads, perceives, or views a particular communication. [*see: communication; sender*]

recommendations

The suggestions or advice in a business report based on the research that has been done. The recommendations are stated at the beginning of an informal report, but at the end of a formal report. [*see: formal report; informal report*]

redundant

a) In communication, words or phrases are redundant or unnecessary when the thoughts or ideas they contain have already been expressed.

b) In business, an employee who is redundant is no longer needed for a particular job and may be dismissed or laid off or transferred to another department or branch.

references

A prospective employer may ask you for references—the names of people who know you well and can verify information given on a résumé or job application form as well as answer any other questions (e.g., were you a good time-keeper at your last job?). Usually you would give the names of former employers, or anyone (**not** a member of your family) who has known you for several years and who holds a responsible position in the community. Always ask someone's permission to use her/his name as a reference before you do so.

research

Finding sources and collecting and organizing information to answer a specific question or solve a specific problem. [*see: information; sources*]

resources

People and places where you can find information when you do research. For example a library is a resource; the books in the library are sources of information. [*see: research; sources*]

résumé

A document which describes your education and work experience to a prospective employer. Your résumé should list your qualifications, skills, talents, and interests and may also include several references. [*see: references; skill; talent*]

rules of order

The procedures by which formal business meetings are run. Extremely formal meetings are held according to *Robert's Rules of Order* which are based on parliamentary procedures. [*see: amendment; formal meeting; motion*]

sales letter

A letter which is designed and written to attract the receiver's attention and convince her/him to buy a specific product or service.

secondary information

Information that someone else has previously researched and recorded, and which you find useful in your own research of a particular topic (e.g., information you find in an encyclopaedia). [*see: primary information*]

secretary

The person responsible for keeping the records of a company or organization. (*see: agenda; minutes of a meeting; notice of a meeting*]

sender

The person who transmits a particular communication; the source of the communication. [*see: communication; message; receiver*]

service business

A company which does not manufacture products but which performs work or provides assistance. For example, accounting and dry-cleaning are service businesses. [*see: manufacturing*]

simple listing

A method of arranging your message by listing items/topics in alphabetical or numerical order. [*see: organizer*]

skill

The ability to perform a task. A skill is something which must be learned; it is not something which you have from the day you are born. For example, you may be a "born dancer," but you have to learn the skills involved in the specific steps of a particular dance. [*see: résumé; talent*]

skim-reading

When you skim-read, you move your eyes quickly over written

material to find only the most essential and most important facts. [*see: reading rate; reading with concentration*]

sources
People and "objects" (such as books, films, and magazines) where you can find information when you are doing research. [*see: bibliography; resources*]

spatial order
A way of describing how objects are arranged within a certain space. [*see: organizer*]

subjective
Being influenced by personal opinions or feelings in situations, including when sending or receiving messages.

subordinates
People of lesser rank or authority than you in a company. [*see: peers*]

summary
The section of a formal business report in which the main ideas from the body of the report are stated. The summary may also include a brief explanation of the major recommendations or conclusions. [*see: conclusion; formal report; main idea; recommendations*]

symbol
A visual representation of an idea or object; a form of non-verbal communication.

table of contents
A list of the sections and subsections and the corresponding page numbers in a lengthy written communication, such as a book or report. [*see: formal report*]

talent
A special ability to perform a task. A talent is not something you can learn—it is something with which you are born. [*see: résumé; skill*]

technical language
Words used to describe specialized areas of knowledge. For example, auto mechanics and computer processors have their own technical language; this glossary contains many of the

technical words necessary to study business communications. [*see: jargon*]

technical manual
A reference book which contains the specifications of and instructions for a machine or piece of equipment.

time order
A system of arranging items into the order in which they happened; or of listing tasks in the order in which they should be performed. [*see: organizer*]

title page
The first page of a formal business report which includes: the title of the report, the names of the people who prepared it and for whom it was prepared, and the date. [*see: formal report*]

training seminar
A classroom situation in which a small group of people receives intensive instruction in a particular subject or job.

treasurer
The person at a business meeting who is responsible for the finances of the company or organization (e.g., membership fees).

typo
Short for **typographical error**—a mistake in typing or keyboarding. Typos are marked on written material using proofreader's marks, and subsequently corrected. [*see: proofreader's marks; proofreading*]

verbal
Having to do with words (e.g. speaking and writing).

voice control
How you use your voice when you are speaking, regardless of what you are saying. Voice control includes **clarity, intonation, pace, pitch, voice quality,** and **volume**. [*see: the individual entries for each in this glossary; non-verbal communication*]

voice quality

The description of how your voice sounds (e.g., warm, resonant, thin, harsh). It is determined by the length of the vocal cords and the degree of tension in the neck muscles. [*see: voice control*]

volume

The degree of loudness of your voice. [*see: voice-control*]

volunteer work

A job or service you perform for which you are unpaid. For someone with little or no work experience, volunteer work can be an important source to draw on for skills, achievements, and references when applying for jobs. [*see: résumé*]

voting

Used to decide whether a motion is carried or defeated at a formal business meeting. The participants may use a voice vote, a show of hands, or a ballot vote to indicate whether or not they accept a proposal. At company meetings, voting is not done in secret. [*see: formal meeting; motion*]

working environment

The physical surroundings and conditions in which a job is performed (e.g., outdoors/indoors, temperature, ventilation, noise level).

ACKNOWLEDGEMENTS

These acknowledgements are an extension of the copyright page. Every effort has been made to determine the copyright holders. In the case of omission, the publishers will be pleased to make suitable acknowledgements in future editions.

Page 32	Excerpt from *The Edge*, Ontario Ministry of Skills Development, © Queen's Printer for Ontario, 1986.
Page 42	Excerpt from *SL-1 User Guide* reprinted courtesy of Telecommunications Terminal Systems (TTS).
Page 65	Excerpt from "Hazardous Hobbies," *Canadian Consumer*. 16. no. 1 (January 1986). Reprinted courtesy of the Consumers' Association of Canada. More consumer information is available in *Canadian Consumer* magazine: Consumers' Association of Canada, Box 9300, Ottawa, Ontario, K1G 3T9.
Page 65	Excerpt from *Anne and Jay* by Barbara Bartholomew. Reprinted by permission of New American Library.
Page 66	"Perception of Stress Key to Handling it Psychologist Says" reprinted by permission of *The Canadian Press*.
Page 71	Amy Wohl: "WP Software: the status of compatibility," from *Office Equipment & Methods* (Jan./Feb. 1986). Reprinted courtesy of Maclean Hunter.
Page 73	"Bell Labs Brings Fiber-Optic Phones Closer to Home." Reprinted from the March 17, 1986 issue of *Business Week* by special permission, © 1986 by McGraw-Hill, Inc.
Page 76	Excerpts from *In Search of Excellence: Lessons from America's Best-Run Companies* by Thomas J. Peters and Robert H. Waterman, Jr. Copyright © 1982 by Thomas J. Peters and Robert H. Waterman, Jr. Reprinted by permission of Harper & Row, Publishers, Inc.
Page 120	Excerpt from *Fat Paper: Diets for Trimming Paperwork* by Lee Grossman. Copyright © 1976 by McGraw-Hill, Inc. Reproduced by permission of the publishers.
Page 144	"Test Your Telephone Habits" reproduced by permission of Bell Canada.
Page 225	Laura C. Johnson and Jeffrey G. Reitz: *Youth Unemployment in Metropolitan Toronto*. Reprinted by permission of the Social Planning Council of Metropolitan Toronto.

Photos and Illustrations

Page 18	Crombie McNeil/Game Plan
Page 18	Bob Burch/Game Plan
Page 18	C. John Moore
Page 18	National Film Board of Canada
Page 18, 26	Randy Richmond; courtesy of *The Nanticoke Times*
Pages 18, 22, 39, 85, 140, 147, 149, 150, 155, 182, 202	Muriel Fiona Napier
Pages 22, 84, 206	Brian Lister, AV Technician, Timothy Eaton Secondary School
Page 26	Metropolitan Toronto Police Force
Page 27, 61, 130	Ministry of Transportation and Communications
Page 28	Air Canada
Page 28	Canadian Broadcasting Corporation
Page 28	McDonald's Restaurants of Canada Ltd.
Page 28	Shell Canada Limited
Pages 69, 74, 182, 202, 204	Randy Richmond; courtesy of Toronto Public Library
Page 72	Hewlett-Packard (Canada) Ltd.
Page 73	Bell Cellular
Page 85	Canadian Hearing Society
Page 105	Olivetti Canada Ltd.
Page 128	Bank of Montreal
Page 129	Employment and Immigration Canada
Page 137	Tony Marshall
Page 137	Global Television Network
Page 136	Karen Clark; courtesy of Metropolitan Toronto Police Force
Page 139	Karen Clark
Page 142	Bell Canada Telephone Historical Collection
Page 142	Northern Telecom
Page 202	The Globe and Mail
Page 202	Institute of Canadian Advertising
Page 202	The Toronto Star
Page 202	Bell and Howell

With thanks to the staff and students of Timothy Eaton Secondary School and the staff of Oxford University Press Canada.

Page 8	Drabble cartoon—Reprinted by permission of United Feature Syndicate, Inc.
Page 45	Nestlings cartoon — Reprinted by permission of Warren Clements.
Page 61	The "Bizarro" cartoon is reprinted by permission of Chronicle Features, San Francisco.
Pages 64, 101	Shoe cartoons — Reprinted by permission: Tribune Media Services.
Page 68	Auth cartoon—Copyright 1984, *Philadelphia Inquirer*. Reprinted with permission of Universal Press Syndicate. All rights reserved.
Pages 82, 146, 200	Peanuts cartoon—Reprinted by permission of United Feature Syndicate, Inc.
Page 156	Elwood cartoon — Reprinted by permission: Tribune Media Services.
Page 184	On the Fastrack cartoon—Reprinted by permission of King Features Syndicate.

INDEX